THE STORY OF MY LIFE
AND
THE WORLD I LIVE IN

by

Helen Keller

GP

GRINDL PRESS

This edition contains the manuscripts of *The Story Of My Life* and *The World I Live In*, by Helen Keller. All content not in the public domain in the United States, is original to this edition. Content in the public domain in the United States includes the novel manuscripts and all photographic images.

The Story Of My Life manuscript originally published 1903
The World I Live In manuscript originally published 1908

Copyright © 2013 by C. Wade Nancy

All rights reserved. No part of the original content or design of this book may be reproduced in any form or by any means, electronic or mechanical. Printed in the United States of America.

ISBN:

GP
GRINDL PRESS
grindlpress.com

This book is one of numerous titles in the
CLASSIC BIOGRAPHY SERIES
available from Grindl Press.

Other Classic Literature Series and Titles from Grindl Press
grindlpress.com

SECONDARY EDUCATION EDITIONS

Heart of Darkness

Ethan Frome

Gulliver's Travels: A Voyage to Lilliput and A Voyage to Brobdingnag

Gulliver's Travels: In Four Parts

Fathers and Sons

The Red Badge of Courage

Candide

The Scarlet Letter

VOCABULARY FROM THE CLASSICS SERIES

Increase Vocabulary by Reading Franz Kafka's *Metamorphosis*

Increase Vocabulary by Reading Voltaire's *Candide*

ETHNIC STUDIES SERIES

Narrative of the Life of Frederick Douglass an American Slave

My Bondage and My Freedom

The Souls of Black Folk

The Negro

Autobiography of Black Hawk

Up From Slavery

THE STORY OF MY LIFE

To Alexander Graham Bell

Who has taught the deaf to speak and enabled the listening ear to hear speech from the Atlantic to the Rockies, I dedicate this **Story of My Life.**

CONTENTS

Chapter I 1	Chapter XIII 30
Chapter II 4	Chapter XIV 33
Chapter III 8	Chapter XV..................38
Chapter IV 10	Chapter XVI 41
Chapter V 12	Chapter XVII 42
Chapter VI 14	Chapter XVIII............44
Chapter VII.................. 16	Chapter XIX............... 47
Chapter VIII 20	Chapter XX 50
Chapter IX 21	Chapter XXI 55
Chapter X....................24	Chapter XXII 63
Chapter XI 25	Chapter XXIII 70
Chapter XII.................28	

THE WORLD I LIVE IN 77

Special to this 2013 edition:
Helen Keller Through the Years (photos)....................... 76

Chapter I

IT IS with a kind of fear that I begin to write the history of my life. I have, as it were, a superstitious hesitation in lifting the veil that clings about my childhood like a golden mist. The task of writing an autobiography is a difficult one. When I try to classify my earliest impressions, I find that fact and fancy look alike across the years that link the past with the present. The woman paints the child's experiences in her own fantasy. A few impressions stand out vividly from the first years of my life; but "the shadows of the prison-house are on the rest." Besides, many of the joys and sorrows of childhood have lost their poignancy; and many incidents of vital importance in my early education have been forgotten in the excitement of great discoveries. In order, therefore, not to be tedious I shall try to present in a series of sketches only the episodes that seem to me to be the most interesting and important.

I was born on June 27, 1880, in Tuscumbia, a little town of northern Alabama.

The family on my father's side is descended from Caspar Keller, a native of Switzerland, who settled in Maryland. One of my Swiss ancestors was the first teacher of the deaf in Zurich and wrote a book on the subject of their education—rather a singular coincidence; though it is true that there is no king who has not had a slave among his ancestors, and no slave who has not had a king among his.

My grandfather, Caspar Keller's son, "entered" large tracts of land in Alabama and finally settled there. I have been told that once a year he went from Tuscumbia to Philadelphia on horseback to purchase supplies for the plantation, and my aunt has in her possession many of the letters to his family, which give charming and vivid accounts of these trips.

My Grandmother Keller was a daughter of one of Lafayette's aides, Alexander Moore, and granddaughter of Alexander Spotswood, an early Colonial Governor of Virginia. She was also second cousin to Robert E. Lee.

My father, Arthur H. Keller, was a captain in the Confederate Army, and my mother, Kate Adams, was his second wife and many years younger. Her grandfather, Benjamin Adams, married Susanna E. Goodhue, and lived in Newbury, Massachusetts, for many years. Their son, Charles Adams, was born in Newburyport, Massachusetts, and moved to Helena, Arkansas. When the Civil War broke out, he fought on the side of the South and became a brigadier-general. He married Lucy Helen Everett, who belonged to the same family of Everetts as Edward Everett and Dr. Edward Everett Hale. After the war was over the family moved to Memphis, Tennessee.

I lived, up to the time of the illness that deprived me of my sight and hearing, in a tiny house consisting of a large square room and a small one, in which the servant slept. It is a custom in the South to build a small house near the homestead as an annex to be used on occasion. Such a house my father built after the Civil War, and when he married my mother they went to live in it. It was completely covered with vines, climbing roses and honeysuckles. From the garden it looked like an arbour. The little porch was hidden from view by a screen of yellow roses and Southern smilax. It was the favourite haunt of humming-birds and bees.

The Keller homestead, where the family lived, was a few steps from our little rose-bower. It was called "Ivy Green" because the house and the surrounding trees and fences were covered with beautiful English ivy. Its old-fashioned garden was the paradise of my childhood.

Even in the days before my teacher came, I used to feel along the square stiff boxwood hedges, and, guided by the sense of smell would find the first violets and lilies. There, too, after a fit of temper, I went to find comfort and to hide my hot face in the cool leaves and grass. What joy it was to lose myself in that garden of flowers, to wander happily from spot to spot, until, coming suddenly upon a beautiful vine, I recognized it by its leaves and blossoms, and knew it was the vine which covered the tumble-down summer-house at the farther end of the garden! Here, also, were trailing clematis, drooping jessamine, and some rare sweet flowers called butterfly lilies, because their fragile petals resemble butterflies' wings. But the roses—they were loveliest of all. Never have I found in the greenhouses of the North such heart-satisfying roses as the climbing roses of my southern home. They used to hang in long festoons from our porch, filling the whole air with their fragrance, untainted by any earthy smell; and in the early morning, washed in the dew, they felt so soft, so pure, I could not help wondering if they did not resemble the asphodels of God's garden.

The beginning of my life was simple and much like every other little life. I came, I saw, I conquered, as the first baby in the family always does. There was the usual amount of discussion as to a name for me. The first baby in the family was not to be lightly named, every one was emphatic about that. My father suggested the name of Mildred Campbell, an ancestor whom he highly esteemed, and he declined to take any further part in the discussion. My mother solved the problem by giving it as her wish that I should be called after her mother, whose maiden name was Helen Everett. But in the excitement of carrying me to church my father lost the name on the way, very naturally, since it was one in which he had declined to have a part. When the minister asked him for it, he just remembered that it had been decided to call me after my grandmother, and he gave her name as Helen Adams.

I am told that while I was still in long dresses I showed many signs of an eager, self-asserting disposition. Everything that I saw other people do I insisted upon imitating. At six months I could pipe out "How d'ye," and one day I attracted every one's attention by saying "Tea, tea, tea" quite plainly. Even after my illness I remembered one of the words I had learned in these early months. It was the word "water," and I continued to make some sound for that word after all other speech was lost. I ceased making the sound "wah-wah" only when I learned to spell the word.

They tell me I walked the day I was a year old. My mother had just taken me out of the bath-tub and was holding me in her lap, when I was suddenly attracted by the flickering shadows of leaves that danced in the sunlight on the smooth floor. I slipped from my mother's lap and almost ran toward them. The impulse gone, I fell down and cried for her to take me up in her arms.

These happy days did not last long. One brief spring, musical with the song of robin and mocking-bird, one summer rich in fruit and roses, one autumn of gold and crimson sped by and left their gifts at the feet of an eager, delighted child. Then, in the dreary month of February, came the illness which closed my eyes and ears and plunged me into the unconsciousness of a new-born baby. They called it acute congestion of the stomach and brain. The doctor thought I could not live. Early one morning, however, the fever left me as suddenly and mysteriously as it had come. There was great rejoicing in the family that morning, but no one, not even the doctor, knew that I should never see or hear again.

I fancy I still have confused recollections of that illness. I especially remember the tenderness with which my mother tried to soothe me in my waling hours of fret and pain, and the agony and bewilderment with which I awoke after a tossing half sleep, and turned my eyes, so dry and hot, to the wall away from the once-loved light, which came to me dim and yet more dim each day. But, except for these fleeting memories, if, indeed, they be memories, it all seems very unreal, like a nightmare. Gradually I got used to the silence and darkness that surrounded me and forgot that it had ever been different, until she came—my teacher—who was to set my spirit free. But during the first nineteen months of my life I had caught glimpses of broad, green fields, a luminous sky, trees and flowers which the darkness that followed could not wholly blot out. If we have once seen, "the day is ours, and what the day has shown."

Chapter II

I CANNOT recall what happened during the first months after my illness. I only know that I sat in my mother's lap or clung to her dress as she went about her household duties. My hands felt every object and observed every motion, and in this way I learned to know many things. Soon I felt the need of some communication with others and began to make crude signs. A shake of the head meant "No" and a nod, "Yes," a pull meant "Come" and a push, "Go." Was it bread that I wanted? Then I would imitate the acts of cutting the slices and buttering them. If I wanted my mother to make ice-cream for dinner I made the sign for working the freezer and shivered, indicating cold. My mother, moreover, succeeded in making me understand a good deal. I always knew when she wished me to bring her something, and I would run upstairs or anywhere else she indicated. Indeed, I owe to her loving wisdom all that was bright and good in my long night.

I understood a good deal of what was going on about me. At five I learned to fold and put away the clean clothes when they were brought in from the laundry, and I distinguished my own from the rest. I knew by the way my mother and aunt dressed when they were going out, and I invariably begged to go with them. I was always sent for when there was company, and when the guests took their leave, I waved my hand to them, I think with a vague remembrance of the meaning of the gesture. One day some gentlemen called on my mother, and I felt the shutting of the front door and other sounds that indicated their arrival. On a sudden thought I ran upstairs before any one could stop me, to put on my idea of a company dress. Standing before the mirror, as I had seen others do, I anointed mine head with oil and covered my face thickly with powder. Then I pinned a veil over my head so that it covered my face and fell in folds down to my shoulders, and tied an enormous bustle round my small waist, so that it dangled behind, almost meeting the hem of my skirt. Thus attired I went down to help entertain the company.

I do not remember when I first realized that I was different from other people; but I knew it before my teacher came to me. I had noticed that my mother and my friends did not use signs as I did when they wanted anything done, but talked with their mouths. Sometimes I stood between two persons who were conversing and touched their lips. I could not understand, and was vexed. I moved my lips and gesticulated frantically without result. This made me so angry at times that I kicked and screamed until I was exhausted.

I think I knew when I was naughty, for I knew that it hurt Ella, my nurse, to kick her, and when my fit of temper was over I had a feeling akin to regret. But I cannot remember any instance in which this feeling prevented me from repeating the naughtiness when I failed to get what I wanted.

In those days a little coloured girl, Martha Washington, the child of our cook, and Belle, an old setter, and a great hunter in her day, were my constant companions. Martha Washington understood my signs, and I seldom had any difficulty in making her do just as I wished. It pleased me to domineer over her, and she generally submitted to my tyranny rather than risk a hand-to-hand encounter. I was strong, active, indifferent to consequences. I knew my own mind well enough and always had my own way, even if I had to fight tooth and nail for it. We spent a great deal of time in the kitchen, kneading dough balls, helping make ice-cream, grinding coffee, quarreling over the cake-bowl, and feeding the hens and turkeys that swarmed about the kitchen steps. Many of them were so tame that they would eat from my hand and let me feel them. One big gobbler snatched a tomato from me one day and ran away with it. Inspired, perhaps, by Master Gobbler's success, we carried off to the woodpile a cake which the cook had just frosted, and ate every bit of it. I was quite ill afterward, and I wonder if retribution also overtook the turkey.

The guinea-fowl likes to hide her nest in out-of-the-way places, and it was one of my greatest delights to hunt for the eggs in the long grass. I could not tell Martha Washington when I wanted to go egg-hunting, but I would double my hands and put them on the ground, which meant something round in the grass, and Martha always understood. When we were fortunate enough to find a nest I never allowed her to carry the eggs home, making her understand by emphatic signs that she might fall and break them.

The sheds where the corn was stored, the stable where the horses were kept, and the yard where the cows were milked morning and evening were unfailing sources of interest to Martha and me. The milkers would let me keep my hands on the cows while they milked, and I often got well switched by the cow for my curiosity.

The making ready for Christmas was always a delight to me. Of course I did not know what it was all about, but I enjoyed the pleasant odours that filled the house and the tidbits that were given to Martha Washington and me to keep us quiet. We were sadly in the way, but that did not interfere with our pleasure in the least. They allowed us to grind the spices, pick over the raisins and lick the stirring spoons. I hung my stocking because the others did; I cannot remember, however, that the ceremony interested me especially, nor did my curiosity cause me to wake before daylight to look for my gifts.

Martha Washington had as great a love of mischief as I. Two little children were seated on the veranda steps one hot July afternoon. One was black as ebony, with little bunches of fuzzy hair tied with shoestrings sticking out all over her head like corkscrews. The other was white, with long golden curls. One child was six years old, the other two or three years older. The younger child was blind—that was I—and the other was Martha Washington. We were busy cutting out paper dolls; but we soon wearied of this amusement, and after cutting up our shoestrings and clipping all the leaves off the honeysuckle that were within reach, I turned my attention to Martha's corkscrews. She objected at first, but finally submitted. Thinking that turn and turn about is fair play, she seized the scissors and cut off one of my curls, and would have cut them all off but for my mother's timely interference.

Belle, our dog, my other companion, was old and lazy and liked to sleep by the open fire rather than to romp with me. I tried hard to teach her my sign language, but she was dull and inattentive. She sometimes started and quivered with excitement, then she became perfectly rigid, as dogs do when they point a bird. I did not then know why Belle acted in this way; but I knew she was not doing as I wished. This vexed me and the lesson always ended in a one-sided boxing match. Belle would get up, stretch herself lazily, give one or two contemptuous sniffs, go to the opposite side of the hearth and lie down again, and I, wearied and disappointed, went off in search of Martha.

Many incidents of those early years are fixed in my memory, isolated, but clear and distinct, making the sense of that silent, aimless, dayless life all the more intense.

One day I happened to spill water on my apron, and I spread it out to dry before the fire which was flickering on the sitting-room hearth. The apron did not dry quickly enough to suit me, so I drew nearer and threw it right over the hot ashes. The fire leaped into life; the flames encircled me so that in a moment my clothes were blazing. I made a terrified noise that brought Viny, my old nurse, to the rescue. Throwing a blanket over me, she almost suffocated me, but she put out the fire. Except for my hands and hair I was not badly burned.

About this time I found out the use of a key. One morning I locked my mother up in the pantry, where she was obliged to remain three hours, as the servants were in a detached part of the house. She kept pounding on the door, while I sat outside on the porch steps and laughed with glee as I felt the jar of the pounding. This most naughty prank of mine convinced my parents that I must be taught as soon as possible. After my teacher, Miss Sullivan, came to me, I sought an early opportunity to lock her in her room. I went upstairs with something which my mother made me understand I was to give to Miss Sullivan; but no sooner had I given it to her than I slammed the door to, locked it, and hid the key under the wardrobe in the hall. I could not be induced to tell where the key was. My father was obliged to get a ladder and take Miss Sullivan out through the window—much to my delight. Months after I produced the key.

When I was about five years old we moved from the little vine-covered house to a large new one. The family consisted of my father and mother, two older half-brothers, and, afterward, a little sister, Mildred. My earliest distinct recollection of my father is making my way through great drifts of newspapers to his side and finding him alone, holding a sheet of paper before his face. I was greatly puzzled to know what he was doing. I imitated this action, even wearing his spectacles, thinking they might help solve the mystery. But I did not find out the secret for several years. Then I learned what those papers were, and that my father edited one of them.

My father was most loving and indulgent, devoted to his home, seldom leaving us, except in the hunting season. He was a great hunter, I have been told, and a celebrated shot. Next to his family he loved his dogs and gun. His hospitality was great, almost to a fault, and he seldom came home without bringing a guest. His special pride was the big garden where, it was said, he raised the finest watermelons and strawberries in the county; and to me he brought the first ripe grapes and the choicest berries. I remember his caressing touch as he led me from tree to tree, from vine to vine, and his eager delight in whatever pleased me.

He was a famous story-teller; after I had acquired language he used to spell clumsily into my hand his cleverest anecdotes, and nothing pleased him more than to have me repeat them at an opportune moment.

I was in the North, enjoying the last beautiful days of the summer of 1896, when I heard the news of my father's death. He had had a short illness, there had been a brief time of acute suffering, then all was over. This was my first great sorrow—my first personal experience with death.

How shall I write of my mother? She is so near to me that it almost seems indelicate to speak of her.

For a long time I regarded my little sister as an intruder. I knew that

I had ceased to be my mother's only darling, and the thought filled me with jealousy. She sat in my mother's lap constantly, where I used to sit, and seemed to take up all her care and time. One day something happened which seemed to me to be adding insult to injury.

At that time I had a much-petted, much-abused doll, which I afterward named Nancy. She was, alas, the helpless victim of my outbursts of temper and of affection, so that she became much the worse for wear. I had dolls which talked, and cried, and opened and shut their eyes; yet I never loved one of them as I loved poor Nancy. She had a cradle, and I often spent an hour or more rocking her. I guarded both doll and cradle with the most jealous care; but once I discovered my little sister sleeping peacefully in the cradle. At this presumption on the part of one to whom as yet no tie of love bound me I grew angry. I rushed upon the cradle and over-turned it, and the baby might have been killed had my mother not caught her as she fell. Thus it is that when we walk in the valley of twofold solitude we know little of the tender affections that grow out of endearing words and actions and companionship. But afterward, when I was restored to my human heritage, Mildred and I grew into each other's hearts, so that we were content to go hand-in-hand wherever caprice led us, although she could not understand my finger language, nor I her childish prattle.

⇒ Chapter III ⇐

MEANWHILE THE desire to express myself grew. The few signs I used became less and less adequate, and my failures to make myself understood were invariably followed by outbursts of passion. I felt as if invisible hands were holding me, and I made frantic efforts to free myself. I struggled—not that struggling helped matters, but the spirit of resistance was strong within me; I generally broke down in tears and physical exhaustion. If my mother happened to be near I crept into her arms, too miserable even to remember the cause of the tempest. After awhile the need of some means of communication became so urgent that these outbursts occurred daily, sometimes hourly.

My parents were deeply grieved and perplexed. We lived a long way from any school for the blind or the deaf, and it seemed unlikely that any one would come to such an out-of-the-way place as Tuscumbia to teach a child who was both deaf and blind. Indeed, my friends and relatives sometimes doubted whether I could be taught. My mother's only ray of hope came from Dickens's "American Notes." She had read his account of Laura Bridgman, and remembered vaguely that she was deaf and blind, yet had been educated. But she also remembered with a hopeless pang that Dr. Howe, who had discovered the way to teach the deaf and blind, had been dead many years. His methods had probably died with him; and if they had not, how was a little girl in a far-off town in Alabama to receive the benefit of them?

When I was about six years old, my father heard of an eminent oculist in Baltimore, who had been successful in many cases that had seemed hopeless. My parents at once determined to take me to Baltimore to see if anything could be done for my eyes.

The journey, which I remember well was very pleasant. I made friends with many people on the train. One lady gave me a box of shells. My father made holes in these so that I could string them, and for a long time they kept me happy and contented. The conductor, too, was kind. Often when he went his rounds I clung to his coat tails while he collected and punched the tickets. His punch, with which he let me play, was a delightful toy. Curled up in a corner of the seat I amused myself for hours making funny little holes in bits of cardboard.

My aunt made me a big doll out of towels. It was the most comical shapeless thing, this improvised doll, with no nose, mouth, ears or eyes—nothing that even the imagination of a child could convert into a face. Curiously enough, the absence of eyes struck me more than all the other defects put together. I pointed this out to everybody with provoking persistency, but no one seemed equal to the task of providing the doll with eyes. A bright idea, however, shot into my mind, and the problem was solved. I tumbled off the seat and searched under it until I found my aunt's cape, which was trimmed with large beads. I pulled two beads off and indicated to her that I wanted her to sew them on my doll. She raised my hand to her eyes in a questioning way, and I nodded energetically. The beads were sewed in the right place and I could not contain myself for joy; but immediately I lost all interest in the doll. During the whole trip I did not have one fit of temper, there were so many things to keep my mind and fingers busy.

When we arrived in Baltimore, Dr. Chisholm received us kindly: but he could do nothing. He said, however, that I could be educated, and advised my father to consult Dr. Alexander Graham Bell of Washington, who would be able to give him information about schools and teachers of deaf or blind children. Acting on the doctor's advice, we went immediately to Washington to see Dr. Bell, my father with a sad heart and many misgivings, I wholly unconscious of his anguish, finding pleasure in the excitement of moving from place to place. Child as I was, I at once felt the tenderness and sympathy which endeared Dr. Bell to so many hearts, as his wonderful achievements enlist their admiration. He held me on his knee while I examined his watch, and he made it strike for me. He understood my signs, and I knew it and loved him at once. But I did not dream that that interview would be the door through which I should pass from darkness into light, from isolation to friendship, companionship, knowledge, love.

Dr. Bell advised my father to write to Mr. Anagnos, director of the Perkins Institution in Boston, the scene of Dr. Howe's great labours for the blind, and ask him if he had a teacher competent to begin my education. This my father did at once, and in a few weeks there came a kind letter from Mr. Anagnos with the comforting assurance that a teacher had been found. This was in the summer of 1886. But Miss Sullivan did not arrive until the following March.

Thus I came up out of Egypt and stood before Sinai, and a power divine touched my spirit and gave it sight, so that I beheld many wonders. And from the sacred mountain I heard a voice which said, "Knowledge is love and light and vision."

⇒ Chapter IV ⇐

THE MOST important day I remember in all my life is the one on which my teacher, Anne Mansfield Sullivan, came to me. I am filled with wonder when I consider the immeasurable contrasts between the two lives which it connects. It was the third of March, 1887, three months before I was seven years old.

On the afternoon of that eventful day, I stood on the porch, dumb, expectant. I guessed vaguely from my mother's signs and from the hurrying to and fro in the house that something unusual was about to happen, so I went to the door and waited on the steps. The afternoon sun penetrated the mass of honeysuckle that covered the porch, and fell on my upturned face. My fingers lingered almost unconsciously on the familiar leaves and blossoms which had just come forth to greet the sweet southern spring. I did not know what the future held of marvel or surprise for me. Anger and bitterness had preyed upon me continually for weeks and a deep languor had succeeded this passionate struggle.

Have you ever been at sea in a dense fog, when it seemed as if a tangible white darkness shut you in, and the great ship, tense and anxious, groped her way toward the shore with plummet and sounding-line, and you waited with beating heart for something to happen? I was like that ship before my education began, only I was without compass or sounding-line, and had no way of knowing how near the harbour was. "Light! give me light!" was the wordless cry of my soul, and the light of love shone on me in that very hour.

I felt approaching footsteps, I stretched out my hand as I supposed to my mother. Some one took it, and I was caught up and held close in the arms of her who had come to reveal all things to me, and, more than all things else, to love me.

The morning after my teacher came she led me into her room and gave me a doll. The little blind children at the Perkins Institution had sent it and Laura Bridgman had dressed it; but I did not know this until afterward. When I had played with it a little while, Miss Sullivan slowly spelled into my hand the word "d-o-l-l." I was at once interested in this finger play and tried to imitate it. When I finally succeeded in making the letters correctly I was flushed with childish pleasure and pride. Running downstairs to my mother I held up my hand and made the letters for doll. I did not know that I was spelling a word or even that words existed; I was simply making my fingers go in monkey-like imitation. In the days that followed I learned to spell in this uncomprehending way a great many words, among them pin, hat, cup and a few verbs like sit, stand and walk. But my teacher had been with me several weeks before I understood that everything has a name.

One day, while I was playing with my new doll, Miss Sullivan put my big rag doll into my lap also, spelled "d-o-l-l" and tried to make me understand that "d-o-l-l" applied to both. Earlier in the day we had had a tussle over the words "m-u-g" and "w-a-t-e-r." Miss Sullivan had tried to impress it upon me that "m-u-g" is mug and that "w-a-t-e-r" is water, but I persisted in confounding the two. In despair she had dropped the subject for the time, only to renew it at the first opportunity. I became impatient at her repeated attempts and, seizing the new doll, I dashed it upon the floor. I was keenly delighted when I felt the fragments of the broken doll at my feet. Neither sorrow nor regret followed my passionate outburst. I had not loved the doll. In the still, dark world in which I lived there was no strong sentiment or tenderness. I felt my teacher sweep the fragments to one side of the hearth, and I had a sense of satisfaction that the cause of my discomfort was removed. She brought me my hat, and I knew I was going out into the warm sunshine. This thought, if a wordless sensation may be called a thought, made me hop and skip with pleasure.

We walked down the path to the well-house, attracted by the fragrance of the honeysuckle with which it was covered. Some one was drawing water and my teacher placed my hand under the spout. As the cool stream gushed over one hand she spelled into the other the word water, first slowly, then rapidly. I stood still, my whole attention fixed upon the motions of her fingers. Suddenly I felt a misty consciousness as of something forgotten—a thrill of returning thought; and somehow the mystery of language was revealed to me. I knew then that "w-a-t-e-r" meant the wonderful cool something that was flowing over my hand. That living word awakened my soul, gave it light, hope, joy, set it free! There were barriers still, it is true, but barriers that could in time be swept away.

I left the well-house eager to learn. Everything had a name, and each name gave birth to a new thought. As we returned to the house every object which I touched seemed to quiver with life. That was because I saw everything with the strange, new sight that had come to me. On entering the door I remembered the doll I had broken. I felt my way to the hearth and picked up the pieces. I tried vainly to put them together. Then my eyes filled with tears; for I realized what I had done, and for the first time I felt repentance and sorrow.

I learned a great many new words that day. I do not remember what they all were; but I do know that mother, father, sister, teacher were among them—words that were to make the world blossom for me, "like Aaron's rod, with flowers." It would have been difficult to find a happier child than I was as I lay in my crib at the close of that eventful day and lived over the joys it had brought me, and for the first time longed for a new day to come.

⇒ Chapter V ⇐

I RECALL many incidents of the summer of 1887 that followed my soul's sudden awakening. I did nothing but explore with my hands and learn the name of every object that I touched; and the more I handled things and learned their names and uses, the more joyous and confident grew my sense of kinship with the rest of the world.

When the time of daisies and buttercups came Miss Sullivan took me by the hand across the fields, where men were preparing the earth for the seed, to the banks of the Tennessee River, and there, sitting on the warm grass, I had my first lessons in the beneficence of nature. I learned how the sun and the rain make to grow out of the ground every tree that is pleasant to the sight and good for food, how birds build their nests and live and thrive from land to land, how the squirrel, the deer, the lion and every other creature finds food and shelter. As my knowledge of things grew I felt more and more the delight of the world I was in. Long before I learned to do a sum in arithmetic or describe the shape of the earth, Miss Sullivan had taught me to find beauty in the fragrant woods, in every blade of grass, and in the curves and dimples of my baby sister's hand. She linked my earliest thoughts with nature, and made me feel that "birds and flowers and I were happy peers."

But about this time I had an experience which taught me that nature is not always kind. One day my teacher and I were returning from a long ramble. The morning had been fine, but it was growing warm and sultry when at last we turned our faces homeward. Two or three times we stopped to rest under a tree by the wayside. Our last halt was under a wild cherry tree a short distance from the house. The shade was grateful, and the tree was so easy to climb that with my teacher's assistance I was able to scramble to a seat in the branches. It was so cool up in the tree that Miss Sullivan proposed that we have our luncheon there. I promised to keep still while she went to the house to fetch it.

Suddenly a change passed over the tree. All the sun's warmth left the air. I knew the sky was black, because all the heat, which meant light to me, had died out of the atmosphere. A strange odour came up from the earth. I knew it, it was the odour that always precedes a thunderstorm, and a nameless fear clutched at my heart. I felt absolutely alone, cut off from my friends and the firm earth. The immense, the unknown, enfolded me. I remained still and expectant; a chilling terror crept over me. I longed for my teacher's return; but above all things I wanted to get down from that tree.

There was a moment of sinister silence, then a multitudinous stirring of the leaves. A shiver ran through the tree, and the wind sent forth a blast that would have knocked me off had I not clung to the branch with might and main. The tree swayed and strained. The small twigs snapped and fell about me in showers. A wild impulse to jump seized me, but terror held me fast. I crouched down in the fork of the tree. The branches lashed about me. I felt the intermittent jarring that came now and then, as if something heavy had fallen and the shock had traveled up till it reached the limb I sat on. It worked my suspense up to the highest point, and just as I was thinking the tree and I should fall together, my teacher seized my hand and helped me down. I clung to her, trembling with joy to feel the earth under my feet once more. I had learned a new lesson—that nature "wages open war against her children, and under softest touch hides treacherous claws."

After this experience it was a long time before I climbed another tree. The mere thought filled me with terror. It was the sweet allurement of the mimosa tree in full bloom that finally overcame my fears. One beautiful spring morning when I was alone in the summer-house, reading, I became aware of a wonderful subtle fragrance in the air. I started up and instinctively stretched out my hands. It seemed as if the spirit of spring had passed through the summer-house. "What is it?" I asked, and the next minute I recognized the odour of the mimosa blossoms. I felt my way to the end of the garden, knowing that the mimosa tree was near the fence, at the turn of the path. Yes, there it was, all quivering in the warm sunshine, its blossom-laden branches almost touching the long grass. Was there ever anything so exquisitely beautiful in the world before! Its delicate blossoms shrank from the slightest earthly touch; it seemed as if a tree of paradise had been transplanted to earth. I made my way through a shower of petals to the great trunk and for one minute stood irresolute; then, putting my foot in the broad space between the forked branches, I pulled myself up into the tree. I had some difficulty in holding on, for the branches were very large and the bark hurt my hands. But I had a delicious sense that I was doing something unusual and wonderful so I kept on climbing higher and higher, until I reached a little seat which somebody had built there so long ago that it had grown part of the tree itself. I sat there for a long, long time, feeling like a fairy on a rosy cloud. After that I spent many happy hours in my tree of paradise, thinking fair thoughts and dreaming bright dreams.

⇒ Chapter VI ⇐

I HAD now the key to all language, and I was eager to learn to use it. Children who hear acquire language without any particular effort; the words that fall from others' lips they catch on the wing, as it were, delightedly, while the little deaf child must trap them by a slow and often painful process. But whatever the process, the result is wonderful. Gradually from naming an object we advance step by step until we have traversed the vast distance between our first stammered syllable and the sweep of thought in a line of Shakespeare.

At first, when my teacher told me about a new thing I asked very few questions. My ideas were vague, and my vocabulary was inadequate; but as my knowledge of things grew, and I learned more and more words, my field of inquiry broadened, and I would return again and again to the same subject, eager for further information. Sometimes a new word revived an image that some earlier experience had engraved on my brain.

I remember the morning that I first asked the meaning of the word, "love." This was before I knew many words. I had found a few early violets in the garden and brought them to my teacher. She tried to kiss me: but at that time I did not like to have any one kiss me except my mother. Miss Sullivan put her arm gently round me and spelled into my hand, "I love Helen."

"What is love?" I asked.

She drew me closer to her and said, "It is here," pointing to my heart, whose beats I was conscious of for the first time. Her words puzzled me very much because I did not then understand anything unless I touched it.

I smelt the violets in her hand and asked, half in words, half in signs, a question which meant, "Is love the sweetness of flowers?"

"No," said my teacher.

Again I thought. The warm sun was shining on us.

"Is this not love?" I asked, pointing in the direction from which the heat came. "Is this not love?"

It seemed to me that there could be nothing more beautiful than the sun, whose warmth makes all things grow. But Miss Sullivan shook her head, and I was greatly puzzled and disappointed. I thought it strange that my teacher could not show me love.

A day or two afterward I was stringing beads of different sizes in symmetrical groups—two large beads, three small ones, and so on. I had made many mistakes, and Miss Sullivan had pointed them out again and again with gentle patience. Finally I noticed a very obvious error in the sequence and for an instant I concentrated my attention on the lesson and tried to think how I should have arranged the beads. Miss Sullivan touched my forehead and spelled with decided emphasis, "Think."

In a flash I knew that the word was the name of the process that was going on in my head. This was my first conscious perception of an abstract idea.

For a long time I was still—I was not thinking of the beads in my lap, but trying to find a meaning for "love" in the light of this new idea. The sun had been under a cloud all day, and there had been brief showers; but suddenly the sun broke forth in all its southern splendour.

Again I asked my teacher, "Is this not love?"

"Love is something like the clouds that were in the sky before the sun came out," she replied. Then in simpler words than these, which at that time I could not have understood, she explained: "You cannot touch the clouds, you know; but you feel the rain and know how glad the flowers and the thirsty earth are to have it after a hot day. You cannot touch love either; but you feel the sweetness that it pours into everything. Without love you would not be happy or want to play."

The beautiful truth burst upon my mind—I felt that there were invisible lines stretched between my spirit and the spirits of others.

From the beginning of my education Miss Sullivan made it a practice to speak to me as she would speak to any hearing child; the only difference was that she spelled the sentences into my hand instead of speaking them. If I did not know the words and idioms necessary to express my thoughts she supplied them, even suggesting conversation when I was unable to keep up my end of the dialogue.

This process was continued for several years; for the deaf child does not learn in a month, or even in two or three years, the numberless idioms and expressions used in the simplest daily intercourse. The little hearing child learns these from constant repetition and imitation. The conversation he hears in his home stimulates his mind and suggests topics and calls forth the spontaneous expression of his own thoughts. This natural exchange of ideas is denied to the deaf child. My teacher, realizing this, determined to supply the kinds of stimulus I lacked. This she did by repeating to me as far as possible, verbatim, what she heard, and by showing me how I could take part in the conversation. But it was a long time before I ventured to take the initiative, and still longer before I could find something appropriate to say at the right time.

The deaf and the blind find it very difficult to acquire the amenities of conversation. How much more this difficulty must be augmented in the case of those who are both deaf and blind! They cannot distinguish the tone of the voice or, without assistance, go up and down the gamut of tones that give significance to words; nor can they watch the expression of the speaker's face, and a look is often the very soul of what one says.

⇒ Chapter VII ⇐

THE NEXT important step in my education was learning to read.

As soon as I could spell a few words my teacher gave me slips of cardboard on which were printed words in raised letters. I quickly learned that each printed word stood for an object, an act, or a quality. I had a frame in which I could arrange the words in little sentences; but before I ever put sentences in the frame I used to make them in objects. I found the slips of paper which represented, for example, "doll," "is," "on," "bed" and placed each name on its object; then I put my doll on the bed with the words is, on, bed arranged beside the doll, thus making a sentence of the words, and at the same time carrying out the idea of the sentence with the things themselves.

One day, Miss Sullivan tells me, I pinned the word girl on my pinafore and stood in the wardrobe. On the shelf I arranged the words, is, in, wardrobe. Nothing delighted me so much as this game. My teacher and I played it for hours at a time. Often everything in the room was arranged in object sentences.

From the printed slip it was but a step to the printed book. I took my "Reader for Beginners" and hunted for the words I knew; when I found them my joy was like that of a game of hide-and-seek. Thus I began to read. Of the time when I began to read connected stories I shall speak later.

For a long time I had no regular lessons. Even when I studied most earnestly it seemed more like play than work. Everything Miss Sullivan taught me she illustrated by a beautiful story or a poem. Whenever anything delighted or interested me she talked it over with me just as if she were a little girl herself. What many children think of with dread, as a painful plodding through grammar, hard sums and harder definitions, is to-day one of my most precious memories.

I cannot explain the peculiar sympathy Miss Sullivan had with my pleasures and desires. Perhaps it was the result of long association with the blind. Added to this she had a wonderful faculty for description. She went quickly over uninteresting details, and never nagged me with questions to see if I remembered the day-before-yesterday's lesson. She introduced dry technicalities of science little by little, making every subject so real that I could not help remembering what she taught.

We read and studied out of doors, preferring the sunlit woods to the house. All my early lessons have in them the breath of the woods—the fine, resinous odour of pine needles, blended with the perfume of wild grapes. Seated in the gracious shade of a wild tulip tree, I learned to think that everything has a lesson and a suggestion. "The loveliness of things taught me all their use." Indeed, everything that could hum, or buzz, or sing, or bloom had a part in my education-noisy-throated frogs, katydids and crickets held in my hand until forgetting their embarrassment, they trilled their reedy note, little downy chickens and wildflowers, the dogwood blossoms, meadow-violets and budding fruit trees. I felt the bursting cotton-bolls and fingered their soft fiber and fuzzy seeds; I felt the low soughing of the wind through the cornstalks, the silky rustling of the long leaves, and the indignant snort of my pony, as we caught him in the pasture and put the bit in his mouth—ah me! how well I remember the spicy, clovery smell of his breath!

Sometimes I rose at dawn and stole into the garden while the heavy dew lay on the grass and flowers. Few know what joy it is to feel the roses pressing softly into the hand, or the beautiful motion of the lilies as they sway in the morning breeze. Sometimes I caught an insect in the flower I was plucking, and I felt the faint noise of a pair of wings rubbed together in a sudden terror, as the little creature became aware of a pressure from without.

Another favourite haunt of mine was the orchard, where the fruit ripened early in July. The large, downy peaches would reach themselves into my hand, and as the joyous breezes flew about the trees the apples tumbled at my feet. Oh, the delight with which I gathered up the fruit in my pinafore, pressed my face against the smooth cheeks of the apples, still warm from the sun, and skipped back to the house!

Our favourite walk was to Keller's Landing, an old tumbledown lumber-wharf on the Tennessee River, used during the Civil War to land soldiers. There we spent many happy hours and played at learning geography. I built dams of pebbles, made islands and lakes, and dug river-beds, all for fun, and never dreamed that I was learning a lesson. I listened with increasing wonder to Miss Sullivan's descriptions of the great round world with its burning mountains, buried cities, moving rivers of ice, and many other things as strange. She made raised maps in clay, so that I could feel the mountain ridges and valleys, and follow with my fingers the devious course of rivers. I liked this, too; but the division of the earth into zones and poles confused and teased my mind. The illustrative strings and the orange stick representing the poles seemed so real that even to this day the mere mention of temperate zone suggests a series of twine circles; and I believe that if any one should set about it he could convince me that white bears actually climb the North Pole.

Arithmetic seems to have been the only study I did not like. From the first I was not interested in the science of numbers. Miss Sullivan tried to teach me to count by stringing beads in groups, and by arranging kintergarten straws I learned to add and subtract. I never had patience to arrange more than five or six groups at a time. When I had accomplished this my conscience was at rest for the day, and I went out quickly to find my playmates.

In this same leisurely manner I studied zoology and botany.

Once a gentleman, whose name I have forgotten, sent me a collection of fossils—tiny mollusk shells beautifully marked, and bits of sandstone with the print of birds' claws, and a lovely fern in bas-relief. These were the keys which unlocked the treasures of the antediluvian world for me. With trembling fingers I listened to Miss Sullivan's descriptions of the terrible beasts, with uncouth, unpronounceable names, which once went tramping through the primeval forests, tearing down the branches of gigantic trees for food, and died in the dismal swamps of an unknown age. For a long time these strange creatures haunted my dreams, and this gloomy period formed a somber background to the joyous Now, filled with sunshine and roses and echoing with the gentle beat of my pony's hoof.

Another time a beautiful shell was given me, and with a child's surprise and delight I learned how a tiny mollusk had built the lustrous coil for his dwelling place, and how on still nights, when there is no breeze stirring the waves, the Nautilus sails on the blue waters of the Indian Ocean in his "ship of pearl." After I had learned a great many interesting things about the life and habits of the children of the sea—how in the midst of dashing waves the little polyps build the beautiful coral isles of the Pacific, and the foraminifera have made the chalk-hills of many a land—my teacher read me "The Chambered Nautilus," and showed me that the shell-building process of the mollusks is symbolical of the development of the mind. Just as the wonder-working mantle of the Nautilus changes the material it absorbs from the water and makes it a part of itself, so the bits of knowledge one gathers undergo a similar change and become pearls of thought.

Again, it was the growth of a plant that furnished the text for a lesson. We bought a lily and set it in a sunny window. Very soon the green, pointed buds showed signs of opening. The slender, fingerlike leaves on the outside opened slowly, reluctant, I thought, to reveal the loveliness they hid; once having made a start, however, the opening process went on rapidly, but in order and systematically. There was always one bud larger and more beautiful than the rest, which pushed her outer, covering back with more pomp, as if the beauty in soft, silky robes knew that she was the lily-queen by right divine, while her more timid sisters doffed their green hoods shyly, until the whole plant was one nodding bough of loveliness and fragrance.

Once there were eleven tadpoles in a glass globe set in a window full of plants. I remember the eagerness with which I made discoveries about them. It was great fun to plunge my hand into the bowl and feel the tadpoles frisk about, and to let them slip and slide between my fingers. One day a more ambitious fellow leaped beyond the edge of the bowl and fell on the floor, where I found him to all appearance more dead than alive. The only sign of life was a slight wriggling of his tail. But no sooner had he returned to his element than he darted to the bottom, swimming round and round in joyous activity. He had made his leap, he had seen the great world, and was content to stay in his pretty glass house under the big fuchsia tree until he attained the dignity of froghood. Then he went to live in the leafy pool at the end of the garden, where he made the summer nights musical with his quaint love-song.

Thus I learned from life itself. At the beginning I was only a little mass of possibilities. It was my teacher who unfolded and developed them. When she came, everything about me breathed of love and joy and was full of meaning. She has never since let pass an opportunity to point out the beauty that is in everything, nor has she ceased trying in thought and action and example to make my life sweet and useful.

It was my teacher's genius, her quick sympathy, her loving tact which made the first years of my education so beautiful. It was because she seized the right moment to impart knowledge that made it so pleasant and acceptable to me. She realized that a child's mind is like a shallow brook which ripples and dances merrily over the stony course of its education and reflects here a flower, there a bush, yonder a fleecy cloud; and she attempted to guide my mind on its way, knowing that like a brook it should be fed by mountain streams and hidden springs, until it broadened out into a deep river, capable of reflecting in its placid surface, billowy hills, the luminous shadows of trees and the blue heavens, as well as the sweet face of a little flower.

Any teacher can take a child to the classroom, but not every teacher can make him learn. He will not work joyously unless he feels that liberty is his, whether he is busy or at rest; he must feel the flush of victory and the heart-sinking of disappointment before he takes with a will the tasks distasteful to him and resolves to dance his way bravely through a dull routine of textbooks.

My teacher is so near to me that I scarcely think of myself apart from her. How much of my delight in all beautiful things is innate, and how much is due to her influence, I can never tell. I feel that her being is inseparable from my own, and that the footsteps of my life are in hers. All the best of me belongs to her—there is not a talent, or an aspiration or a joy in me that has not been awakened by her loving touch.

Chapter VIII

THE FIRST Christmas after Miss Sullivan came to Tuscumbia was a great event. Every one in the family prepared surprises for me, but what pleased me most, Miss Sullivan and I prepared surprises for everybody else. The mystery that surrounded the gifts was my greatest delight and amusement. My friends did all they could to excite my curiosity by hints and half-spelled sentences which they pretended to break off in the nick of time. Miss Sullivan and I kept up a game of guessing which taught me more about the use of language than any set lessons could have done. Every evening, seated round a glowing wood fire, we played our guessing game, which grew more and more exciting as Christmas approached.

On Christmas Eve the Tuscumbia schoolchildren had their tree, to which they invited me. In the centre of the schoolroom stood a beautiful tree ablaze and shimmering in the soft light, its branches loaded with strange, wonderful fruit. It was a moment of supreme happiness. I danced and capered round the tree in an ecstasy. When I learned that there was a gift for each child, I was delighted, and the kind people who had prepared the tree permitted me to hand the presents to the children. In the pleasure of doing this, I did not stop to look at my own gifts; but when I was ready for them, my impatience for the real Christmas to begin almost got beyond control. I knew the gifts I already had were not those of which friends had thrown out such tantalizing hints, and my teacher said the presents I was to have would be even nicer than these. I was persuaded, however, to content myself with the gifts from the tree and leave the others until morning.

That night, after I had hung my stocking, I lay awake a long time, pretending to be asleep and keeping alert to see what Santa Claus would do when he came. At last I fell asleep with a new doll and a white bear in my arms. Next morning it was I who waked the whole family with my first "Merry Christmas!" I found surprises, not in the stocking only, but on the table, on all the chairs, at the door, on the very window-sill; indeed, I could hardly walk without stumbling on a bit of Christmas wrapped up in tissue paper. But when my teacher presented me with a canary, my cup of happiness overflowed.

Little Tim was so tame that he would hop on my finger and eat candied cherries out of my hand. Miss Sullivan taught me to take all the care of my new pet. Every morning after breakfast I prepared his bath, made his cage clean and sweet, filled his cups with fresh seed and water from the well-house, and hung a spray of chickweed in his swing.

One morning I left the cage on the window-seat while I went to fetch water for his bath. When I returned I felt a big cat brush past me as I opened the door. At first I did not realize what had happened; but when I put my hand in the cage and Tim's pretty wings did not meet my touch or his small pointed claws take hold of my finger, I knew that I should never see my sweet little singer again.

⇒ Chapter IX ⇐

THE NEXT important event in my life was my visit to Boston, in May, 1888. As if it were yesterday I remember the preparations, the departure with my teacher and my mother, the journey, and finally the arrival in Boston. How different this journey was from the one I had made to Baltimore two years before! I was no longer a restless, excitable little creature, requiring the attention of everybody on the train to keep me amused. I sat quietly beside Miss Sullivan, taking in with eager interest all that she told me about what she saw out of the car window: the beautiful Tennessee River, the great cotton-fields, the hills and woods, and the crowds of laughing negroes at the stations, who waved to the people on the train and brought delicious candy and popcorn balls through the car. On the seat opposite me sat my big rag doll, Nancy, in a new gingham dress and a beruffled sunbonnet, looking at me out of two bead eyes. Sometimes, when I was not absorbed in Miss Sullivan's descriptions, I remembered Nancy's existence and took her up in my arms, but I gener-ally calmed my conscience by making myself believe that she was asleep.

As I shall not have occasion to refer to Nancy again, I wish to tell here a sad experience she had soon after our arrival in Boston. She was covered with dirt—the remains of mud pies I had compelled her to eat, although she had never shown any special liking for them. The laundress at the Perkins Institution secretly carried her off to give her a bath. This was too much for poor Nancy. When I next saw her she was a formless heap of cotton, which I should not have recognized at all except for the two bead eyes which looked out at me reproachfully.

When the train at last pulled into the station at Boston it was as if a beautiful fairy tale had come true. The "once upon a time" was now; the "far-away country" was here.

We had scarcely arrived at the Perkins Institution for the Blind when I began to make friends with the little blind children. It delighted me inexpressibly to find that they knew the manual alphabet. What joy to talk with other children in my own language! Until then I had been like a foreigner speaking through an interpreter. In the school where Laura Bridgman was taught I was in my own country. It took me some time to appreciate the fact that my new friends were blind. I knew I could not see; but it did not seem possible that all the eager, loving children who gathered round me and joined heartily in my frolics were also blind. I remember the surprise and the pain I felt as I noticed that they placed their hands over mine when I talked to them and that they read books with their fingers. Although I had been told this before, and although I understood my own deprivations, yet I had thought vaguely that since they could hear, they must have a sort of "second sight," and I was not prepared to find one child and another and yet another deprived of the same precious gift. But they were so happy and contented that I lost all sense of pain in the pleasure of their companionship.

One day spent with the blind children made me feel thoroughly at home in my new environment, and I looked eagerly from one pleasant experience to another as the days flew swiftly by. I could not quite convince myself that there was much world left, for I regarded Boston as the beginning and the end of creation.

While we were in Boston we visited Bunker Hill, and there I had my first lesson in history. The story of the brave men who had fought on the spot where we stood excited me greatly. I climbed the monument, counting the steps, and wondering as I went higher and yet higher if the soldiers had climbed this great stairway and shot at the enemy on the ground below.

The next day we went to Plymouth by water. This was my first trip on the ocean and my first voyage in a steamboat. How full of life and motion it was! But the rumble of the machinery made me think it was thundering, and I began to cry, because I feared if it rained we should not be able to have our picnic out of doors. I was more interested, I think, in the great rock on which the Pilgrims landed than in anything else in Plymouth. I could touch it, and perhaps that made the coming of the Pilgrims and their toils and great deeds seem more real to me. I have often held in my hand a little model of the Plymouth Rock which a kind gentleman gave me at Pilgrim Hall, and I have fingered its curves, the split in the centre and the embossed figures "1620," and turned over in my mind all that I knew about the wonderful story of the Pilgrims.

How my childish imagination glowed with the splendour of their enterprise! I idealized them as the bravest and most generous men that ever sought a home in a strange land. I thought they desired the freedom of their fellow men as well as their own. I was keenly surprised and disappointed years later to learn of their acts of persecution that make us tingle with shame, even while we glory in the courage and energy that gave us our "Country Beautiful."

Among the many friends I made in Boston were Mr. William Endicott and his daughter. Their kindness to me was the seed from which many pleasant memories have since grown. One day we visited their beautiful home at Beverly Farms. I remember with delight how I went through their rose-garden, how their dogs, big Leo and little curly-haired Fritz with long ears, came to meet me, and how Nimrod, the swiftest of the horses, poked his nose into my hands for a pat and a lump of sugar. I also remember the beach, where for the first time I played in the sand. It was hard, smooth sand, very different from the loose, sharp sand, mingled with kelp and shells, at Brewster. Mr. Endicott told me about the great ships that came sailing by from Boston, bound for Europe. I saw him many times after that, and he was always a good friend to me; indeed, I was thinking of him when I called Boston "the City of Kind Hearts."

≈ Chapter X ≈

JUST BEFORE the Perkins Institution closed for the summer, it was arranged that my teacher and I should spend our vacation at Brewster, on Cape Cod, with our dear friend, Mrs. Hopkins. I was delighted, for my mind was full of the prospective joys and of the wonderful stories I had heard about the sea.

My most vivid recollection of that summer is the ocean. I had always lived far inland and had never had so much as a whiff of salt air; but I had read in a big book called "Our World" a description of the ocean which filled me with wonder and an intense longing to touch the mighty sea and feel it roar. So my little heart leaped high with eager excitement when I knew that my wish was at last to be realized.

No sooner had I been helped into my bathing-suit than I sprang out upon the warm sand and without thought of fear plunged into the cool water. I felt the great billows rock and sink. The buoyant motion of the water filled me with an exquisite, quivering joy. Suddenly my ecstasy gave place to terror; for my foot struck against a rock and the next instant there was a rush of water over my head. I thrust out my hands to grasp some support, I clutched at the water and at the seaweed which the waves tossed in my face. But all my frantic efforts were in vain. The waves seemed to be playing a game with me, and tossed me from one to another in their wild frolic. It was fearful! The good, firm earth had slipped from my feet, and everything seemed shut out from this strange, all-enveloping element—life, air, warmth and love. At last, however, the sea, as if weary of its new toy, threw me back on the shore, and in another instant I was clasped in my teacher's arms. Oh, the comfort of the long, tender embrace! As soon as I had recovered from my panic sufficiently to say anything, I demanded: "Who put salt in the water?"

After I had recovered from my first experience in the water, I thought it great fun to sit on a big rock in my bathing-suit and feel wave after wave dash against the rock, sending up a shower of spray which quite covered me. I felt the pebbles rattling as the waves threw their ponderous weight against the shore; the whole beach seemed racked by their terrific onset, and the air throbbed with their pulsations. The breakers would swoop back to gather themselves for a mightier leap, and I clung to the rock, tense, fascinated, as I felt the dash and roar of the rushing sea!

I could never stay long enough on the shore. The tang of the untainted, fresh and free sea air was like a cool, quieting thought, and the shells and pebbles and the seaweed with tiny living creatures attached to it never lost their fascination for me. One day Miss Sullivan attracted my attention to a strange object which she had captured basking in the shallow water. It was a great horseshoe crab—the first one I had ever seen. I felt of him and thought it very strange that he should carry his house on his back. It suddenly occurred to me that he might make a delightful pet; so I seized him by the tail with both hands and carried him home. This feat pleased me highly, as his body was very heavy, and it took all my strength to drag him half a mile. I would not leave Miss Sullivan in peace until she had put the crab in a trough near the well where I was confident he would be secure. But next morning I went to the trough, and lo, he had disappeared! Nobody knew where he had gone, or how he had escaped. My disappointment was bitter at the time; but little by little I came to realize that it was not kind or wise to force this poor dumb creature out of his element, and after awhile I felt happy in the thought that perhaps he had returned to the sea.

Chapter XI

IN THE autumn I returned to my Southern home with a heart full of joyous memories. As I recall that visit North I am filled with wonder at the richness and variety of the experiences that cluster about it. It seems to have been the beginning of everything. The treasures of a new, beautiful world were laid at my feet, and I took in pleasure and information at every turn. I lived myself into all things. I was never still a moment; my life was as full of motion as those little insects that crowd a whole existence into one brief day. I met many people who talked with me by spelling into my hand, and thought in joyous sympathy leaped up to meet thought, and behold, a miracle had been wrought! The barren places between my mind and the minds of others blossomed like the rose.

I spent the autumn months with my family at our summer cottage, on a mountain about fourteen miles from Tuscumbia. It was called Fern Quarry, because near it there was a limestone quarry, long since abandoned. Three frolicsome little streams ran through it from springs in the rocks above, leaping here and tumbling there in laughing cascades wherever the rocks tried to bar their way. The opening was filled with ferns which completely covered the beds of limestone and in places hid the streams. The rest of the mountain was thickly wooded. Here were great oaks and splendid evergreens with trunks like mossy pillars, from the branches of which hung garlands of ivy and mistletoe, and persimmon trees, the odour of which pervaded every nook and corner of the wood—an illusive, fragrant something that made the heart glad. In places the wild muscadine and scuppernong vines stretched from tree to tree, making arbours which were always full of butterflies and buzzing insects. It was delightful to lose ourselves in the green hollows of that tangled wood in the late afternoon, and to smell the cool, delicious odours that came up from the earth at the close of day.

Our cottage was a sort of rough camp, beautifully situated on the top of the mountain among oaks and pines. The small rooms were arranged on each side of a long open hall. Round the house was a wide piazza, where the mountain winds blew, sweet with all wood-scents. We lived on the piazza most of the time—there we worked, ate and played. At the back door there was a great butternut tree, round which the steps had been built, and in front the trees stood so close that I could touch them and feel the wind shake their branches, or the leaves twirl downward in the autumn blast.

Many visitors came to Fern Quarry. In the evening, by the campfire, the men played cards and whiled away the hours in talk and sport. They told stories of their wonderful feats with fowl, fish and quadruped—how many wild ducks and turkeys they had shot, what "savage trout" they had caught, and how they had bagged the craftiest foxes, outwitted the most clever 'possums and overtaken the fleetest deer, until I thought that surely the lion, the tiger, the bear and the rest of the wild tribe would not be able to stand before these wily hunters. "To-morrow to the chase!" was their good-night shout as the circle of merry friends broke up for the night. The men slept in the hall outside our door, and I could feel the deep breathing of the dogs and the hunters as they lay on their improvised beds.

At dawn I was awakened by the smell of coffee, the rattling of guns, and the heavy footsteps of the men as they strode about, promising themselves the greatest luck of the season. I could also feel the stamping of the horses, which they had ridden out from town and hitched under the trees, where they stood all night, neighing loudly, impatient to be off. At last the men mounted, and, as they say in the old songs, away went the steeds with bridles ringing and whips cracking and hounds racing ahead, and away went the champion hunters "with hark and whoop and wild halloo!"

Later in the morning we made preparations for a barbecue. A fire was kindled at the bottom of a deep hole in the ground, big sticks were laid crosswise at the top, and meat was hung from them and turned on spits. Around the fire squatted negroes, driving away the flies with long branches. The savoury odour of the meat made me hungry long before the tables were set.

When the bustle and excitement of preparation was at its height, the hunting party made its appearance, struggling in by twos and threes, the men hot and weary, the horses covered with foam, and the jaded hounds panting and dejected—and not a single kill! Every man declared that he had seen at least one deer, and that the animal had come very close; but however hotly the dogs might pursue the game, however well the guns might be aimed, at the snap of the trigger there was not a deer in sight. They had been as fortunate as the little boy who said he came very near seeing a rabbit—he saw his tracks. The party soon forgot its disappointment, however, and we sat down, not to venison, but to a tamer feast of veal and roast pig.

One summer I had my pony at Fern Quarry. I called him Black Beauty, as I had just read the book, and he resembled his namesake in every way, from his glossy black coat to the white star on his forehead. I spent many of my happiest hours on his back. Occasionally, when it was quite safe, my teacher would let go the leading-rein, and the pony sauntered on or stopped at his sweet will to eat grass or nibble the leaves of the trees that grew beside the narrow trail.

On mornings when I did not care for the ride, my teacher and I would start after breakfast for a ramble in the woods, and allow ourselves to get lost amid the trees and vines, with no road to follow except the paths made by cows and horses. Frequently we came upon impassable thickets which forced us to take a round about way. We always returned to the cottage with armfuls of laurel, goldenrod, ferns and gorgeous swamp-flowers such as grow only in the South.

Sometimes I would go with Mildred and my little cousins to gather persimmons. I did not eat them; but I loved their fragrance and enjoyed hunting for them in the leaves and grass. We also went nutting, and I helped them open the chestnut burrs and break the shells of hickory-nuts and walnuts—the big, sweet walnuts!

At the foot of the mountain there was a railroad, and the children watched the trains whiz by. Sometimes a terrific whistle brought us to the steps, and Mildred told me in great excitement that a cow or a horse had strayed on the track. About a mile distant there was a trestle spanning a deep gorge. It was very difficult to walk over, the ties were wide apart and so narrow that one felt as if one were walking on knives. I had never crossed it until one day Mildred, Miss Sullivan and I were lost in the woods, and wandered for hours without finding a path.

Suddenly Mildred pointed with her little hand and exclaimed, "There's the trestle!" We would have taken any way rather than this; but it was late and growing dark, and the trestle was a short cut home. I had to feel for the rails with my toe; but I was not afraid, and got on very well, until all at once there came a faint "puff, puff" from the distance.

"I see the train!" cried Mildred, and in another minute it would have been upon us had we not climbed down on the crossbraces while it rushed over our heads. I felt the hot breath from the engine on my face, and the smoke and ashes almost choked us. As the train rumbled by, the trestle shook and swayed until I thought we should be dashed to the chasm below. With the utmost difficulty we regained the track. Long after dark we reached home and found the cottage empty; the family were all out hunting for us.

Chapter XII

AFTER MY first visit to Boston, I spent almost every winter in the North. Once I went on a visit to a New England village with its frozen lakes and vast snow fields. It was then that I had opportunities such as had never been mine to enter into the treasures of the snow.

I recall my surprise on discovering that a mysterious hand had stripped the trees and bushes, leaving only here and there a wrinkled leaf. The birds had flown, and their empty nests in the bare trees were filled with snow. Winter was on hill and field. The earth seemed benumbed by his icy touch, and the very spirits of the trees had withdrawn to their roots, and there, curled up in the dark, lay fast asleep. All life seemed to have ebbed away, and even when the sun shone the day was

> *Shrunk and cold,*
> *As if her veins were sapless and old,*
> *And she rose up decrepitly*
> *For a last dim look at earth and sea.*

The withered grass and the bushes were transformed into a forest of icicles.

Then came a day when the chill air portended a snowstorm. We rushed out-of-doors to feel the first few tiny flakes descending. Hour by hour the flakes dropped silently, softly from their airy height to the earth, and the country became more and more level. A snowy night closed upon the world, and in the morning one could scarcely recognize a feature of the landscape. All the roads were hidden, not a single landmark was visible, only a waste of snow with trees rising out of it.

In the evening a wind from the northeast sprang up, and the flakes rushed hither and thither in furious melee. Around the great fire we sat and told merry tales, and frolicked, and quite forgot that we were in the midst of a desolate solitude, shut in from all communication with the outside world. But during the night the fury of the wind increased to such a degree that it thrilled us with a vague terror. The rafters creaked and strained, and the branches of the trees surrounding the house rattled and beat against the windows, as the winds rioted up and down the country.

On the third day after the beginning of the storm the snow ceased. The sun broke through the clouds and shone upon a vast, undulating white plain. High mounds, pyramids heaped in fantastic shapes, and impenetrable drifts lay scattered in every direction.

Narrow paths were shoveled through the drifts. I put on my cloak and hood and went out. The air stung my cheeks like fire. Half walking in the paths, half working our way through the lesser drifts, we succeeded in reaching a pine grove just outside a broad pasture. The trees stood motionless and white like figures in a marble frieze. There was no odour of pine-needles. The rays of the sun fell upon the trees, so that the twigs sparkled like diamonds and dropped in showers when we touched them. So dazzling was the light, it penetrated even the darkness that veils my eyes.

As the days wore on, the drifts gradually shrunk, but before they were wholly gone another storm came, so that I scarcely felt the earth under my feet once all winter. At intervals the trees lost their icy covering, and the bulrushes and underbrush were bare; but the lake lay frozen and hard beneath the sun.

Our favourite amusement during that winter was tobboganing. In places the shore of the lake rises abruptly from the water's edge. Down these steep slopes we used to coast. We would get on our toboggan, a boy would give us a shove, and off we went! Plunging through drifts, leaping hollows, swooping down upon the lake, we would shoot across its gleaming surface to the opposite bank. What joy! What exhilarating madness! For one wild, glad moment we snapped the chain that binds us to earth, and joining hands with the winds we felt ourselves divine!

Chapter XIII

IT WAS in the spring of 1890 that I learned to speak. The impulse to utter audible sounds had always been strong within me. I used to make noises, keeping one hand on my throat while the other hand felt the movements of my lips. I was pleased with anything that made a noise and liked to feel the cat purr and the dog bark. I also liked to keep my hand on a singer's throat, or on a piano when it was being played. Before I lost my sight and hearing, I was fast learning to talk, but after my illness it was found that I had ceased to speak because I could not hear. I used to sit in my mother's lap all day long and keep my hands on her face because it amused me to feel the motions of her lips; and I moved my lips, too, although I had forgotten what talking was. My friends say that I laughed and cried naturally, and for awhile I made many sounds and word-elements, not because they were a means of communication, but because the need of exercising my vocal organs was imperative. There was, however, one word the meaning of which I still remembered, *water*. I pronounced it "wa-wa." Even this became less and less intelligible until the time when Miss Sullivan began to teach me. I stopped using it only after I had learned to spell the word on my fingers.

I had known for a long time that the people about me used a method of communication different from mine; and even before I knew that a deaf child could be taught to speak, I was conscious of dissatisfaction with the means of communication I already possessed. One who is entirely dependent upon the manual alphabet has always a sense of restraint, of narrowness. This feeling began to agitate me with a vexing, forward-reaching sense of a lack that should be filled. My thoughts would often rise and beat up like birds against the wind, and I persisted in using my lips and voice. Friends tried to discourage this tendency, fearing lest it would lead to disappointment. But I persisted, and an accident soon occurred which resulted in the breaking down of this great barrier—I heard the story of Ragnhild Kaata.

In 1890 Mrs. Lamson, who had been one of Laura Bridgman's teachers, and who had just returned from a visit to Norway and Sweden, came to see me, and told me of Ragnhild Kaata, a deaf and blind girl in Norway who had actually been taught to speak. Mrs. Lamson had scarcely finished telling me about this girl's success before I was on fire with eagerness. I resolved that I, too, would learn to speak. I would not rest satisfied until my teacher took me, for advice and assistance, to Miss Sarah Fuller, principal of the Horace Mann School. This lovely, sweet-natured lady offered to teach me herself, and we began the twenty-sixth of March, 1890.

Miss Fuller's method was this: she passed my hand lightly over her face, and let me feel the position of her tongue and lips when she made a sound. I was eager to imitate every motion and in an hour had learned six elements of speech: M, P, A, S, T, I. Miss Fuller gave me eleven lessons in all. I shall never forget the surprise and delight I felt when I uttered my first connected sentence, "It is warm." True, they were broken and stammering syllables; but they were human speech. My soul, conscious of new strength, came out of bondage, and was reaching through those broken symbols of speech to all knowledge and all faith.

No deaf child who has earnestly tried to speak the words which he has never heard—to come out of the prison of silence, where no tone of love, no song of bird, no strain of music ever pierces the stillness—can forget the thrill of surprise, the joy of discovery which came over him when he uttered his first word. Only such a one can appreciate the eagerness with which I talked to my toys, to stones, trees, birds and dumb animals, or the delight I felt when at my call Mildred ran to me or my dogs obeyed my commands. It is an unspeakable boon to me to be able to speak in winged words that need no interpretation. As I talked, happy thoughts fluttered up out of my words that might perhaps have struggled in vain to escape my fingers.

But it must not be supposed that I could really talk in this short time. I had learned only the elements of speech. Miss Fuller and Miss Sullivan could understand me, but most people would not have understood one word in a hundred. Nor is it true that, after I had learned these elements, I did the rest of the work myself. But for Miss Sullivan's genius, untiring perseverance and devotion, I could not have progressed as far as I have toward natural speech. In the first place, I laboured night and day before I could be understood even by my most intimate friends; in the second place, I needed Miss Sullivan's assistance constantly in my efforts to articulate each sound clearly and to combine all sounds in a thousand ways. Even now she calls my attention every day to mispronounced words.

All teachers of the deaf know what this means, and only they can at all appreciate the peculiar difficulties with which I had to contend. In reading my teacher's lips I was wholly dependent on my fingers: I had to use the sense of touch in catching the vibrations of the throat, the movements of the mouth and the expression of the face; and often this sense was at fault. In such cases I was forced to repeat the words or sentences, sometimes for hours, until I felt the proper ring in my own voice. My work was practice, practice, practice. Discouragement and weariness cast me down frequently; but the next moment the thought that I should soon be at home and show my loved ones what I had accomplished, spurred me on, and I eagerly looked forward to their pleasure in my achievement.

"My little sister will understand me now," was a thought stronger than all obstacles. I used to repeat ecstatically, "I am not dumb now." I could not be despondent while I anticipated the delight of talking to my mother and reading her responses from her lips. It astonished me to find how much easier it is to talk than to spell with the fingers, and I discarded the manual alphabet as a medium of communication on my part; but Miss Sullivan and a few friends still use it in speaking to me, for it is more convenient and more rapid than lip-reading.

Just here, perhaps, I had better explain our use of the manual alphabet, which seems to puzzle people who do not know us. One who reads or talks to me spells with his hand, using the single-hand manual alphabet generally employed by the deaf. I place my hand on the hand of the speaker so lightly as not to impede its movements. The position of the hand is as easy to feel as it is to see. I do not feel each letter any more than you see each letter separately when you read. Constant practice makes the fingers very flexible, and some of my friends spell rapidly—about as fast as an expert writes on a typewriter. The mere spelling is, of course, no more a conscious act than it is in writing.

When I had made speech my own, I could not wait to go home. At last the happiest of happy moments arrived. I had made my homeward journey, talking constantly to Miss Sullivan, not for the sake of talking, but determined to improve to the last minute. Almost before I knew it, the train stopped at the Tuscumbia station, and there on the platform stood the whole family. My eyes fill with tears now as I think how my mother pressed me close to her, speechless and trembling with delight, taking in every syllable that I spoke, while little Mildred seized my free hand and kissed it and danced, and my father expressed his pride and affection in a big silence. It was as if Isaiah's prophecy had been fulfilled in me, "The mountains and the hills shall break forth before you into singing, and all the trees of the field shall clap their hands!"

Chapter XIV

THE WINTER of 1892 was darkened by the one cloud in my childhood's bright sky. Joy deserted my heart, and for a long, long time I lived in doubt, anxiety and fear. Books lost their charm for me, and even now the thought of those dreadful days chills my heart. A little story called "The Frost King," which I wrote and sent to Mr. Anagnos, of the Perkins Institution for the Blind, was at the root of the trouble. In order to make the matter clear, I must set forth the facts connected with this episode, which justice to my teacher and to myself compels me to relate.

I wrote the story when I was at home, the autumn after I had learned to speak. We had stayed up at Fern Quarry later than usual. While we were there, Miss Sullivan had described to me the beauties of the late foliage, and it seems that her descriptions revived the memory of a story, which must have been read to me, and which I must have unconsciously retained. I thought then that I was "making up a story," as children say, and I eagerly sat down to write it before the ideas should slip from me. My thoughts flowed easily; I felt a sense of joy in the composition. Words and images came tripping to my finger ends, and as I thought out sentence after sentence, I wrote them on my braille slate. Now, if words and images come to me without effort, it is a pretty sure sign that they are not the offspring of my own mind, but stray waifs that I regretfully dismiss. At that time I eagerly absorbed everything I read without a thought of authorship, and even now I cannot be quite sure of the boundary line between my ideas and those I find in books. I suppose that is because so many of my impressions come to me through the medium of others' eyes and ears.

When the story was finished, I read it to my teacher, and I recall now vividly the pleasure I felt in the more beautiful passages, and my annoyance at being interrupted to have the pronunciation of a word corrected. At dinner it was read to the assembled family, who were surprised that I could write so well. Some one asked me if I had read it in a book.

This question surprised me very much; for I had not the faintest recollection of having had it read to me. I spoke up and said, "Oh, no, it is my story, and I have written it for Mr. Anagnos."

Accordingly I copied the story and sent it to him for his birthday. It was suggested that I should change the title from "Autumn Leaves" to "The Frost King," which I did. I carried the little story to the post-office myself, feeling as if I were walking on air. I little dreamed how cruelly I should pay for that birthday gift.

Mr. Anagnos was delighted with "The Frost King," and published it in one of the Perkins Institution reports. This was the pinnacle of my happiness, from which I was in a little while dashed to earth. I had been in Boston only a short time when it was discovered that a story similar to "The Frost King," called "The Frost Fairies" by Miss Margaret T. Canby, had appeared before I was born in a book called "Birdie and His Friends." The two stories were so much alike in thought and language that it was evident Miss Canby's story had been read to me, and that mine was—a plagiarism. It was difficult to make me understand this; but when I did understand I was astonished and grieved. No child ever drank deeper of the cup of bitterness than I did. I had disgraced myself; I had brought suspicion upon those I loved best. And yet how could it possibly have happened? I racked my brain until I was weary to recall anything about the frost that I had read before I wrote "The Frost King"; but I could remember nothing, except the common reference to Jack Frost, and a poem for children, "The Freaks of the Frost," and I knew I had not used that in my composition.

At first Mr. Anagnos, though deeply troubled, seemed to believe me. He was unusually tender and kind to me, and for a brief space the shadow lifted. To please him I tried not to be unhappy, and to make myself as pretty as possible for the celebration of Washington's birthday, which took place very soon after I received the sad news.

I was to be Ceres in a kind of masque given by the blind girls. How well I remember the graceful draperies that enfolded me, the bright autumn leaves that wreathed my head, and the fruit and grain at my feet and in my hands, and beneath all the piety of the masque the oppressive sense of coming ill that made my heart heavy.

The night before the celebration, one of the teachers of the Institution had asked me a question connected with "The Frost King," and I was telling her that Miss Sullivan had talked to me about Jack Frost and his wonderful works. Something I said made her think she detected in my words a confession that I did remember Miss Canby's story of "The Frost Fairies," and she laid her conclusions before Mr. Anagnos, although I had told her most emphatically that she was mistaken.

Mr. Anagnos, who loved me tenderly, thinking that he had been deceived, turned a deaf ear to the pleadings of love and innocence. He believed, or at least suspected, that Miss Sullivan and I had deliberately stolen the bright thoughts of another and imposed them on him to win his admiration. I was brought before a court of investigation composed of the teachers and officers of the Institution, and Miss Sullivan was asked to leave me. Then I was questioned and cross-questioned with what seemed to me a determination on the part of my judges to force me to acknowledge that I remembered having had "The Frost Fairies" read to me. I felt in every question the doubt and suspicion that was in their minds, and I felt, too, that a loved friend was looking at me reproachfully, although I could not have put all this into words. The blood pressed about my thumping heart, and I could scarcely speak, except in monosyllables. Even the consciousness that it was only a dreadful mistake did not lessen my suffering, and when at last I was allowed to leave the room, I was dazed and did not notice my teacher's caresses, or the tender words of my friends, who said I was a brave little girl and they were proud of me.

As I lay in my bed that night, I wept as I hope few children have wept. I felt so cold, I imagined I should die before morning, and the thought comforted me. I think if this sorrow had come to me when I was older, it would have broken my spirit beyond repairing. But the angel of forgetfulness has gathered up and carried away much of the misery and all the bitterness of those sad days.

Miss Sullivan had never heard of "The Frost Fairies" or of the book in which it was published. With the assistance of Dr. Alexander Graham Bell, she investigated the matter carefully, and at last it came out that Mrs. Sophia C. Hopkins had a copy of Miss Canby's "Birdie and His Friends" in 1888, the year that we spent the summer with her at Brewster. Mrs. Hopkins was unable to find her copy; but she has told me that at that time, while Miss Sullivan was away on a vacation, she tried to amuse me by reading from various books, and although she could not remember reading "The Frost Fairies" any more than I, yet she felt sure that "Birdie and His Friends" was one of them. She explained the disappearance of the book by the fact that she had a short time before sold her house and disposed of many juvenile books, such as old schoolbooks and fairy tales, and that "Birdie and His Friends" was probably among them.

The stories had little or no meaning for me then; but the mere spelling of the strange words was sufficient to amuse a little child who could do almost nothing to amuse herself; and although I do not recall a single circumstance connected with the reading of the stories, yet I cannot help thinking that I made a great effort to remember the words, with the intention of having my teacher explain them when she returned. One thing is certain, the language was ineffaceably stamped upon my brain, though for a long time no one knew it, least of all myself.

When Miss Sullivan came back, I did not speak to her about "The Frost Fairies," probably because she began at once to read "Little Lord Fauntleroy," which filled my mind to the exclusion of everything else. But the fact remains that Miss Canby's story was read to me once, and that long after I had forgotten it, it came back to me so naturally that I never suspected that it was the child of another mind.

In my trouble I received many messages of love and sympathy. All the friends I loved best, except one, have remained my own to the present time.

Miss Canby herself wrote kindly, "Some day you will write a great story out of your own head, that will be a comfort and help to many." But this kind prophecy has never been fulfilled. I have never played with words again for the mere pleasure of the game. Indeed, I have ever since been tortured by the fear that what I write is not my own. For a long time, when I wrote a letter, even to my mother, I was seized with a sudden feeling of terror, and I would spell the sentences over and over, to make sure that I had not read them in a book. Had it not been for the persistent encouragement of Miss Sullivan, I think I should have given up trying to write altogether.

I have read "The Frost Fairies" since, also the letters I wrote in which I used other ideas of Miss Canby's. I find in one of them, a letter to Mr. Anagnos, dated September 29, 1891, words and sentiments exactly like those of the book. At the time I was writing "The Frost King," and this letter, like many others, contains phrases which show that my mind was saturated with the story. I represent my teacher as saying to me of the golden autumn leaves, "Yes, they are beautiful enough to comfort us for the flight of summer"—an idea direct from Miss Canby's story.

This habit of assimilating what pleased me and giving it out again as my own appears in much of my early correspondence and my first attempts at writing. In a composition which I wrote about the old cities of Greece and Italy, I borrowed my glowing descriptions, with variations, from sources I have forgotten. I knew Mr. Anagnos's great love of antiquity and his enthusiastic appreciation of all beautiful sentiments about Italy and Greece. I therefore gathered from all the books I read every bit of poetry or of history that I thought would give him pleasure. Mr. Anagnos, in speaking of my composition on the cities, has said, "These ideas are poetic in their essence." But I do not understand how he ever thought a blind and deaf child of eleven could have invented them. Yet I cannot think that because I did not originate the ideas, my little composition is therefore quite devoid of interest. It shows me that I could express my appreciation of beautiful and poetic ideas in clear and animated language.

Those early compositions were mental gymnastics. I was learning, as all young and inexperienced persons learn, by assimilation and imitation, to put ideas into words. Everything I found in books that pleased me I retained in my memory, consciously or unconsciously, and adapted it.

The young writer, as Stevenson has said, instinctively tries to copy whatever seems most admirable, and he shifts his admiration with astonishing versatility. It is only after years of this sort of practice that even great men have learned to marshal the legion of words which come thronging through every byway of the mind.

I am afraid I have not yet completed this process. It is certain that I cannot always distinguish my own thoughts from those I read, because what I read becomes the very substance and texture of my mind. Consequently, in nearly all that I write, I produce something which very much resembles the crazy patchwork I used to make when I first learned to sew. This patchwork was made of all sorts of odds and ends—pretty bits of silk and velvet; but the coarse pieces that were not pleasant to touch always predominated. Likewise my compositions are made up of crude notions of my own, inlaid with the brighter thoughts and riper opinions of the authors I have read. It seems to me that the great difficulty of writing is to make the language of the educated mind express our confused ideas, half feelings, half thoughts, when we are little more than bundles of instinctive tendencies. Trying to write is very much like trying to put a Chinese puzzle together. We have a pattern in mind which we wish to work out in words; but the words will not fit the spaces, or, if they do, they will not match the design. But we keep on trying because we know that others have succeeded, and we are not willing to acknowledge defeat.

"There is no way to become original, except to be born so," says Stevenson, and although I may not be original, I hope sometime to outgrow my artificial, periwigged compositions. Then, perhaps, my own thoughts and experiences will come to the surface. Meanwhile I trust and hope and persevere, and try not to let the bitter memory of "The Frost King" trammel my efforts.

So this sad experience may have done me good and set me thinking on some of the problems of composition. My only regret is that it resulted in the loss of one of my dearest friends, Mr. Anagnos.

Since the publication of "The Story of My Life" in the Ladies' Home Journal, Mr. Anagnos has made a statement, in a letter to Mr. Macy, that at the time of the "Frost King" matter, he believed I was innocent. He says, the court of investigation before which I was brought consisted of eight people: four blind, four seeing persons. Four of them, he says, thought I knew that Miss Canby's story had been read to me, and the others did not hold this view. Mr. Anagnos states that he cast his vote with those who were favourable to me.

But, however the case may have been, with whichever side he may have cast his vote, when I went into the room where Mr. Anagnos had so often held me on his knee and, forgetting his many cares, had shared in my frolics, and found there persons who seemed to doubt me, I felt that there was something hostile and menacing in the very atmosphere, and subsequent events have borne out this impression. For two years he seems to have held the belief that Miss Sullivan and I were innocent. Then he evidently retracted his favourable judgment, why I do not know. Nor did I know the details of the investigation. I never knew even the names of the members of the "court" who did not speak to me. I was too excited to notice anything, too frightened to ask questions. Indeed, I could scarcely think what I was saying, or what was being said to me.

I have given this account of the "Frost King" affair because it was important in my life and education; and, in order that there might be no misunderstanding, I have set forth all the facts as they appear to me, without a thought of defending myself or of laying blame on any one.

≽ Chapter XV ≼

THE SUMMER and winter following the "Frost King" incident I spent with my family in Alabama. I recall with delight that home-going. Everything had budded and blossomed. I was happy. "The Frost King" was forgotten.

When the ground was strewn with the crimson and golden leaves of autumn, and the musk-scented grapes that covered the arbour at the end of the garden were turning golden brown in the sunshine, I began to write a sketch of my life—a year after I had written "The Frost King."

I was still excessively scrupulous about everything I wrote. The thought that what I wrote might not be absolutely my own tormented me. No one knew of these fears except my teacher. A strange sensitiveness prevented me from referring to the "Frost King"; and often when an idea flashed out in the course of conversation I would spell softly to her, "I am not sure it is mine." At other times, in the midst of a paragraph I was writing, I said to myself, "Suppose it should be found that all this was written by some one long ago!" An impish fear clutched my hand, so that I could not write any more that day. And even now I sometimes feel the same uneasiness and disquietude. Miss Sullivan consoled and helped me in every way she could think of; but the terrible experience I had passed through left a lasting impression on my mind, the significance of which I am only just beginning to understand. It was with the hope of restoring my self-confidence that she persuaded me to write for the Youth's

Companion a brief account of my life. I was then twelve years old. As I look back on my struggle to write that little story, it seems to me that I must have had a prophetic vision of the good that would come of the undertaking, or I should surely have failed.

I wrote timidly, fearfully, but resolutely, urged on by my teacher, who knew that if I persevered, I should find my mental foothold again and get a grip on my faculties. Up to the time of the "Frost King" episode, I had lived the unconscious life of a little child; now my thoughts were turned inward, and I beheld things invisible. Gradually I emerged from the penumbra of that experience with a mind made clearer by trial and with a truer knowledge of life.

The chief events of the year 1893 were my trip to Washington during the inauguration of President Cleveland, and visits to Niagara and the World's Fair. Under such circumstances my studies were constantly interrupted and often put aside for many weeks, so that it is impossible for me to give a connected account of them.

We went to Niagara in March, 1893. It is difficult to describe my emotions when I stood on the point which overhangs the American Falls and felt the air vibrate and the earth tremble.

It seems strange to many people that I should be impressed by the wonders and beauties of Niagara. They are always asking: "What does this beauty or that music mean to you? You cannot see the waves rolling up the beach or hear their roar. What do they mean to you?" In the most evident sense they mean everything. I cannot fathom or define their meaning any more than I can fathom or define love or religion or goodness.

During the summer of 1893, Miss Sullivan and I visited the World's Fair with Dr. Alexander Graham Bell. I recall with unmixed delight those days when a thousand childish fancies became beautiful realities. Every day in imagination I made a trip round the world, and I saw many wonders from the uttermost parts of the earth—marvels of invention, treasuries of industry and skill and all the activities of human life actually passed under my finger tips.

I liked to visit the Midway Plaisance. It seemed like the "Arabian Nights," it was crammed so full of novelty and interest. Here was the India of my books in the curious bazaar with its Shivas and elephant-gods; there was the land of the Pyramids concentrated in a model Cairo with its mosques and its long processions of camels; yonder were the lagoons of Venice, where we sailed every evening when the city and the fountains were illuminated. I also went on board a Viking ship which lay a short distance from the little craft. I had been on a man-of-war before, in Boston, and it interested me to see, on this Viking ship, how the seaman was once all in all—how he sailed and took storm and calm alike with undaunted heart, and gave chase to whosoever reechoed his cry, "We are of the sea!" and fought with brains and sinews, self-reliant, self-sufficient, instead of being thrust into the background by unintelligent machinery, as Jack is to-day. So it always is—"man only is interesting to man."

At a little distance from this ship there was a model of the Santa Maria, which I also examined. The captain showed me Columbus's cabin and the desk with an hour-glass on it. This small instrument impressed me most because it made me think how weary the heroic navigator must have felt as he saw the sand dropping grain by grain while desperate men were plotting against his life.

Mr. Higinbotham, President of the World's Fair, kindly gave me permission to touch the exhibits, and with an eagerness as insatiable as that with which Pizarro seized the treasures of Peru, I took in the glories of the Fair with my fingers. It was a sort of tangible kaleidoscope, this white city of the West. Everything fascinated me, especially the French bronzes. They were so lifelike, I thought they were angel visions which the artist had caught and bound in earthly forms.

At the Cape of Good Hope exhibit, I learned much about the processes of mining diamonds. Whenever it was possible, I touched the machinery while it was in motion, so as to get a clearer idea how the stones were weighed, cut, and polished. I searched in the washings for a diamond and found it myself—the only true diamond, they said, that was ever found in the United States.

Dr. Bell went everywhere with us and in his own delightful way described to me the objects of greatest interest. In the electrical building we examined the telephones, autophones, phonographs, and other inventions, and he made me understand how it is possible to send a message on wires that mock space and outrun time, and, like Prometheus, to draw fire from the sky. We also visited the anthropological department, and I was much interested in the relics of ancient Mexico, in the rude stone implements that are so often the only record of an age—the simple monuments of nature's unlettered children (so I thought as I fingered them) that seem bound to last while the memorials of kings and sages crumble in dust away—and in the Egyptian mummies, which I shrank from touching. From these relics I learned more about the progress of man than I have heard or read since.

All these experiences added a great many new terms to my vocabulary, and in the three weeks I spent at the Fair I took a long leap from the little child's interest in fairy tales and toys to the appreciation of the real and the earnest in the workaday world.

Chapter XVI

BEFORE OCTOBER, 1893, I had studied various subjects by myself in a more or less desultory manner. I read the histories of Greece, Rome and the United States. I had a French grammar in raised print, and as I already knew some French, I often amused myself by composing in my head short exercises, using the new words as I came across them, and ignoring rules and other technicalities as much as possible. I even tried, without aid, to master the French pronunciation, as I found all the letters and sounds described in the book. Of course this was tasking slender powers for great ends; but it gave me something to do on a rainy day, and I acquired a sufficient knowledge of French to read with pleasure La Fontaine's "Fables," "Le Medecin Malgre Lui" and passages from "Athalie."

I also gave considerable time to the improvement of my speech. I read aloud to Miss Sullivan and recited passages from my favourite poets, which I had committed to memory; she corrected my pronunciation and helped me to phrase and inflect. It was not, however, until October, 1893, after I had recovered from the fatigue and excitement of my visit to the World's Fair, that I began to have lessons in special subjects at fixed hours.

Miss Sullivan and I were at that time in Hulton, Pennsylvania, visiting the family of Mr. William Wade. Mr. Irons, a neighbour of theirs, was a good Latin scholar; it was arranged that I should study under him. I remember him as a man of rare, sweet nature and of wide experience. He taught me Latin grammar principally; but he often helped me in arithmetic, which I found as troublesome as it was uninteresting. Mr. Irons also read with me Tennyson's "In Memoriam." I had read many books before, but never from a critical point of view. I learned for the first time to know an author, to recognize his style as I recognize the clasp of a friend's hand.

At first I was rather unwilling to study Latin grammar. It seemed absurd to waste time analyzing, every word I came across—noun, genitive, singular, feminine—when its meaning was quite plain. I thought I might just as well describe my pet in order to know it—order, vertebrate; division, quadruped; class, mammalia; genus, felinus; species, cat; individual, Tabby. But as I got deeper into the subject, I became more interested, and the beauty of the language delighted me. I often amused myself by reading Latin passages, picking up words I understood and trying to make sense. I have never ceased to enjoy this pastime.

There is nothing more beautiful, I think, than the evanescent fleeting images and sentiments presented by a language one is just becoming familiar with—ideas that flit across the mental sky, shaped and tinted by capricious fancy. Miss Sullivan sat beside me at my lessons, spelling into my hand whatever Mr. Irons said, and looking up new words for me. I was just beginning to read Caesar's "Gallic War" when I went to my home in Alabama.

⇒ Chapter XVII ⇐

IN THE summer of 1894, I attended the meeting at Chautauqua of the American Association to Promote the Teaching of Speech to the Deaf. There it was arranged that I should go to the Wright-Humason School for the Deaf in New York City. I went there in October, 1894, accompanied by Miss Sullivan. This school was chosen especially for the purpose of obtaining the highest advantages in vocal culture and training in lip-reading. In addition to my work in these subjects, I studied, during the two years I was in the school, arithmetic, physical geography, French and German.

Miss Reamy, my German teacher, could use the manual alphabet, and after I had acquired a small vocabulary, we talked together in German whenever we had a chance, and in a few months I could understand almost everything she said. Before the end of the first year I read "Wilhelm Tell" with the greatest delight. Indeed, I think I made more progress in German than in any of my other studies. I found French much more difficult. I studied it with Madame Olivier, a French lady who did not know the manual alphabet, and who was obliged to give her instruction orally. I could not read her lips easily; so my progress was much slower than in German. I managed, however, to read "Le Medecin Malgre Lui" again. It was very amusing but I did not like it nearly so well as "Wilhelm Tell."

My progress in lip-reading and speech was not what my teachers and I had hoped and expected it would be. It was my ambition to speak like other people, and my teachers believed that this could be accomplished; but, although we worked hard and faithfully, yet we did not quite reach our goal. I suppose we aimed too high, and disappointment was therefore inevitable. I still regarded arithmetic as a system of pitfalls. I hung about the dangerous frontier of "guess," avoiding with infinite trouble to myself and others the broad valley of reason. When I was not guessing, I was jumping at conclusions, and this fault, in addition to my dullness, aggravated my difficulties more than was right or necessary.

But although these disappointments caused me great depression at times, I pursued my other studies with unflagging interest, especially physical geography. It was a joy to learn the secrets of nature: how—in the picturesque language of the Old Testament—the winds are made to blow from the four corners of the heavens, how the vapours ascend from the ends of the earth, how rivers are cut out among the rocks, and mountains overturned by the roots, and in what ways man may overcome many forces mightier than himself. The two years in New York were happy ones, and I look back to them with genuine pleasure.

I remember especially the walks we all took together every day in Central Park, the only part of the city that was congenial to me. I never lost a jot of my delight in this great park. I loved to have it described every time I entered it; for it was beautiful in all its aspects, and these aspects were so many that it was beautiful in a different way each day of the nine months I spent in New York.

In the spring we made excursions to various places of interest. We sailed on the Hudson River and wandered about on its green banks, of which Bryant loved to sing. I liked the simple, wild grandeur of the palisades. Among the places I visited were West Point, Tarrytown, the home of Washington Irving, where I walked through "Sleepy Hollow."

The teachers at the Wright-Humason School were always planning how they might give the pupils every advantage that those who hear enjoy—how they might make much of few tendencies and passive memories in the cases of the little ones—and lead them out of the cramping circumstances in which their lives were set.

Before I left New York, these bright days were darkened by the greatest sorrow that I have ever borne, except the death of my father. Mr. John P. Spaulding, of Boston, died in February, 1896. Only those who knew and loved him best can understand what his friendship meant to me. He, who made every one happy in a beautiful, unobtrusive way, was most kind and tender to Miss Sullivan and me. So long as we felt his loving presence and knew that he took a watchful interest in our work, fraught with so many difficulties, we could not be discouraged. His going away left a vacancy in our lives that has never been filled.

Chapter XVIII

IN OCTOBER, 1896, I entered the Cambridge School for Young Ladies, to be prepared for Radcliffe.

When I was a little girl, I visited Wellesley and surprised my friends by the announcement, "Some day I shall go to college—but I shall go to Harvard!" When asked why I would not go to Wellesley, I replied that there were only girls there. The thought of going to college took root in my heart and became an earnest desire, which impelled me to enter into competition for a degree with seeing and hearing girls, in the face of the strong opposition of many true and wise friends. When I left New York the idea had become a fixed purpose; and it was decided that I should go to Cambridge. This was the nearest approach I could get to Harvard and to the fulfillment of my childish declaration.

At the Cambridge School the plan was to have Miss Sullivan attend the classes with me and interpret to me the instruction given.

Of course my instructors had had no experience in teaching any but normal pupils, and my only means of conversing with them was reading their lips. My studies for the first year were English history, English literature, German, Latin, arithmetic, Latin composition and occasional themes. Until then I had never taken a course of study with the idea of preparing for college; but I had been well drilled in English by Miss Sullivan, and it soon became evident to my teachers that I needed no special instruction in this subject beyond a critical study of the books prescribed by the college. I had had, moreover, a good start in French, and received six months' instruction in Latin; but German was the subject with which I was most familiar.

In spite, however, of these advantages, there were serious drawbacks to my progress. Miss Sullivan could not spell out in my hand all that the books required, and it was very difficult to have textbooks embossed in time to be of use to me, although my friends in London and Philadelphia were willing to hasten the work. For a while, indeed, I had to copy my Latin in braille, so that I could recite with the other girls. My instructors soon became sufficiently familiar with my imperfect speech to answer my questions readily and correct mistakes. I could not make notes in class or write exercises; but I wrote all my compositions and translations at home on my typewriter.

Each day Miss Sullivan went to the classes with me and spelled into my hand with infinite patience all that the teachers said. In study hours she had to look up new words for me and read and reread notes and books I did not have in raised print. The tedium of that work is hard to conceive. Frau Grote, my German teacher, and Mr. Gilman, the principal, were the only teachers in the school who learned the finger alphabet to give me instruction. No one realized more fully than dear Frau Grote how slow and inadequate her spelling was. Nevertheless, in the goodness of her heart she laboriously spelled out her instructions to me in special lessons twice a week, to give Miss Sullivan a little rest. But, though everybody was kind and ready to help us, there was only one hand that could turn drudgery into pleasure.

That year I finished arithmetic, reviewed my Latin grammar, and read three chapters of Caesar's "Gallic War." In German I read, partly with my fingers and partly with Miss Sullivan's assistance, Schiller's "Lied von der Glocke" and "Taucher," Heine's "Harzreise," Freytag's "Aus dem Staat Friedrichs des Grossen," Riehl's "Fluch Der Schonheit," Lessing's "Minna von Barnhelm," and Goethe's "Aus meinem Leben." I took the greatest delight in these German books, especially Schiller's wonderful lyrics, the history of Frederick the Great's magnificent achievements and the account of Goethe's life. I was sorry to finish "Die Harzreise," so full of happy witticisms and charming descriptions of vine-clad hills, streams that sing and ripple in the sunshine, and wild regions, sacred to tradition and legend, the gray sisters of a long-vanished, imaginative age—descriptions such as can be given only by those to whom nature is "a feeling, a love and an appetite."

Mr. Gilman instructed me part of the year in English literature. We read together, "As You Like It," Burke's "Speech on Conciliation with America," and Macaulay's "Life of Samuel Johnson." Mr. Gilman's broad views of history and literature and his clever explanations made my work easier and pleasanter than it could have been had I only read notes mechanically with the necessarily brief explanations given in the classes.

Burke's speech was more instructive than any other book on a political subject that I had ever read. My mind stirred with the stirring times, and the characters round which the life of two contending nations centred seemed to move right before me. I wondered more and more, while Burke's masterly speech rolled on in mighty surges of eloquence, how it was that King George and his ministers could have turned a deaf ear to his warning prophecy of our victory and their humiliation. Then I entered into the melancholy details of the relation in which the great statesman stood to his party and to the representatives of the people. I thought how strange it was that such precious seeds of truth and wisdom should have fallen among the tares of ignorance and corruption.

In a different way Macaulay's "Life of Samuel Johnson" was interesting. My heart went out to the lonely man who ate the bread of affliction in Grub Street, and yet, in the midst of toil and cruel suffering of body and soul, always had a kind word, and lent a helping hand to the poor and despised. I rejoiced over all his successes, I shut my eyes to his faults, and wondered, not that he had them, but that they had not crushed or dwarfed his soul. But in spite of Macaulay's brilliancy and his admirable faculty of making the commonplace seem fresh and picturesque, his positiveness wearied me at times, and his frequent sacrifices of truth to effect kept me in a questioning attitude very unlike the attitude of reverence in which I had listened to the Demosthenes of Great Britain.

At the Cambridge school, for the first time in my life, I enjoyed the companionship of seeing and hearing girls of my own age. I lived with several others in one of the pleasant houses connected with the school, the house where Mr. Howells used to live, and we all had the advantage of home life. I joined them in many of their games, even blind man's buff and frolics in the snow; I took long walks with them; we discussed our studies and read aloud the things that interested us. Some of the girls learned to speak to me, so that Miss Sullivan did not have to repeat their conversation.

At Christmas, my mother and little sister spent the holidays with me, and Mr. Gilman kindly offered to let Mildred study in his school. So Mildred stayed with me in Cambridge, and for six happy months we were hardly ever apart. It makes me most happy to remember the hours we spent helping each other in study and sharing our recreation together.

I took my preliminary examinations for Radcliffe from the 29th of June to the 3rd of July in 1897. The subjects I offered were Elementary and Advanced German, French, Latin, English, and Greek and Roman history, making nine hours in all. I passed in everything, and received "honours" in German and English.

Perhaps an explanation of the method that was in use when I took my examinations will not be amiss here. The student was required to pass in sixteen hours—twelve hours being called elementary and four advanced. He had to pass five hours at a time to have them counted. The examination papers were given out at nine o'clock at Harvard and brought to Radcliffe by a special messenger. Each candidate was known, not by his name, but by a number. I was No. 233, but, as I had to use a typewriter, my identity could not be concealed.

It was thought advisable for me to have my examinations in a room by myself, because the noise of the typewriter might disturb the other girls. Mr. Gilman read all the papers to me by means of the manual alphabet. A man was placed on guard at the door to prevent interruption.

The first day I had German. Mr. Gilman sat beside me and read the paper through first, then sentence by sentence, while I repeated the words aloud, to make sure that I understood him perfectly. The papers were difficult, and I felt very anxious as I wrote out my answers on the typewriter. Mr. Gilman spelled to me what I had written, and I made such changes as I thought necessary, and he inserted them. I wish to say here that I have not had this advantage since in any of my examinations. At Radcliffe no one reads the papers to me after they are written, and I have no opportunity to correct errors unless I finish before the time is up. In that case I correct only such mistakes as I can recall in the few minutes allowed, and make notes of these corrections at the end of my paper. If I passed with higher credit in the preliminaries than in the finals, there are two reasons. In the finals, no one read my work over to me, and in the preliminaries I offered subjects with some of which I was in a measure familiar before my work in the Cambridge school; for at the beginning of the year I had passed examinations in English, History, French and German, which Mr. Gilman gave me from previous Harvard papers.

Mr. Gilman sent my written work to the examiners with a certificate that I, candidate No. 233, had written the papers.

All the other preliminary examinations were conducted in the same manner. None of them was so difficult as the first. I remember that the day the Latin paper was brought to us, Professor Schilling came in and informed me I had passed satisfactorily in German. This encouraged me greatly, and I sped on to the end of the ordeal with a light heart and a steady hand.

≽ Chapter XIX ≼

WHEN I began my second year at the Gilman school, I was full of hope and determination to succeed. But during the first few weeks I was confronted with unforeseen difficulties. Mr. Gilman had agreed that that year I should study mathematics principally. I had physics, algebra, geometry, astronomy, Greek and Latin. Unfortunately, many of the books I needed had not been embossed in time for me to begin with the classes, and I lacked important apparatus for some of my studies. The classes I was in were very large, and it was impossible for the teachers to give me special instruction. Miss Sullivan was obliged to read all the books to me, and interpret for the instructors, and for the first time in eleven years it seemed as if her dear hand would not be equal to the task.

It was necessary for me to write algebra and geometry in class and solve problems in physics, and this I could not do until we bought a braille writer, by means of which I could put down the steps and processes of my work. I could not follow with my eyes the geometrical figures drawn on the blackboard, and my only means of getting a clear idea of them was to make them on a cushion with straight and curved wires, which had bent and pointed ends. I had to carry in my mind, as Mr. Keith says in his report, the lettering of the figures, the hypothesis and conclusion, the construction and the process of the proof. In a word, every study had its obstacles. Sometimes I lost all courage and betrayed my feelings in a way I am ashamed to remember, especially as the signs of my trouble were afterward used against Miss Sullivan, the only person of all the kind friends I had there, who could make the crooked straight and the rough places smooth.

Little by little, however, my difficulties began to disappear. The embossed books and other apparatus arrived, and I threw myself into the work with renewed confidence. Algebra and geometry were the only studies that continued to defy my efforts to comprehend them. As I have said before, I had no aptitude for mathematics; the different points were not explained to me as fully as I wished. The geometrical diagrams were particularly vexing because I could not see the relation of the different parts to one another, even on the cushion. It was not until Mr. Keith taught me that I had a clear idea of mathematics.

I was beginning to overcome these difficulties when an event occurred which changed everything.

Just before the books came, Mr. Gilman had begun to remonstrate with Miss Sullivan on the ground that I was working too hard, and in spite of my earnest protestations, he reduced the number of my recitations. At the beginning we had agreed that I should, if necessary, take five years to prepare for college, but at the end of the first year the success of my examinations showed Miss Sullivan, Miss Harbaugh (Mr. Gilman's head teacher), and one other, that I could without too much effort complete my preparation in two years more. Mr. Gilman at first agreed to this; but when my tasks had become somewhat perplexing, he insisted that I was overworked, and that I should remain at his school three years longer. I did not like his plan, for I wished to enter college with my class.

On the seventeenth of November I was not very well, and did not go to school. Although Miss Sullivan knew that my indisposition was not serious, yet Mr. Gilman, on hearing of it, declared that I was breaking down and made changes in my studies which would have rendered it impossible for me to take my final examinations with my class. In the end the difference of opinion between Mr. Gilman and Miss Sullivan resulted in my mother's withdrawing my sister Mildred and me from the

Cambridge school.

After some delay it was arranged that I should continue my studies under a tutor, Mr. Merton S. Keith, of Cambridge. Miss Sullivan and I spent the rest of the winter with our friends, the Chamberlins in Wrentham, twenty-five miles from Boston.

From February to July, 1898, Mr. Keith came out to Wrentham twice a week, and taught me algebra, geometry, Greek and Latin. Miss Sullivan interpreted his instruction.

In October, 1898, we returned to Boston. For eight months Mr. Keith gave me lessons five times a week, in periods of about an hour. He explained each time what I did not understand in the previous lesson, assigned new work, and took home with him the Greek exercises which I had written during the week on my typewriter, corrected them fully, and returned them to me.

In this way my preparation for college went on without interruption. I found it much easier and pleasanter to be taught by myself than to receive instruction in class. There was no hurry, no confusion. My tutor had plenty of time to explain what I did not understand, so I got on faster and did better work than I ever did in school. I still found more difficulty in mastering problems in mathematics than I did in any other of my studies. I wish algebra and geometry had been half as easy as the languages and literature. But even mathematics Mr. Keith made interesting; he succeeded in whittling problems small enough to get through my brain. He kept my mind alert and eager, and trained it to reason clearly, and to seek conclusions calmly and logically, instead of jumping wildly into space and arriving nowhere. He was always gentle and forbearing, no matter how dull I might be, and believe me, my stupidity would often have exhausted the patience of Job.

On the 29th and 30th of June, 1899, I took my final examinations for Radcliffe College. The first day I had Elementary Greek and Advanced Latin, and the second day Geometry, Algebra and Advanced Greek.

The college authorities did not allow Miss Sullivan to read the examination papers to me; so Mr. Eugene C. Vining, one of the instructors at the Perkins Institution for the Blind, was employed to copy the papers for me in American braille. Mr. Vining was a stranger to me, and could not communicate with me, except by writing braille. The proctor was also a stranger, and did not attempt to communicate with me in any way.

The braille worked well enough in the languages, but when it came to geometry and algebra, difficulties arose. I was sorely perplexed, and felt discouraged wasting much precious time, especially in algebra. It is true that I was familiar with all literary braille in common use in this country—English, American, and New York Point; but the various signs and symbols in geometry and algebra in the three systems are very different, and I had used only the English braille in my algebra.

Two days before the examinations, Mr. Vining sent me a braille copy of one of the old Harvard papers in algebra. To my dismay I found that it was in the American notation. I sat down immediately and wrote to Mr. Vining, asking him to explain the signs. I received another paper and a table of signs by return mail, and I set to work to learn the notation. But on the night before the algebra examination, while I was struggling over some very complicated examples, I could not tell the combinations of bracket, brace and radical. Both Mr. Keith and I were distressed and full of forebodings for the morrow; but we went over to the college a little before the examination began, and had Mr. Vining explain more fully the American symbols.

In geometry my chief difficulty was that I had always been accustomed to read the propositions in line print, or to have them spelled into my hand; and somehow, although the propositions were right before me, I found the braille confusing, and could not fix clearly in my mind what I was reading. But when I took up algebra I had a harder time still. The signs, which I had so lately learned, and which I thought I knew, perplexed me. Besides, I could not see what I wrote on my typewriter. I had always done my work in braille or in my head. Mr. Keith had relied too much on my ability to solve problems mentally, and had not trained me to write examination papers. Consequently my work was painfully slow, and I had to read the examples over and over before I could form any idea of what I was required to do. Indeed, I am not sure now that I read all the signs correctly. I found it very hard to keep my wits about me.

But I do not blame any one. The administrative board of Radcliffe did not realize how difficult they were making my examinations, nor did they understand the peculiar difficulties I had to surmount. But if they unintentionally placed obstacles in my way, I have the consolation of knowing that I overcame them all.

Chapter XX

THE STRUGGLE for admission to college was ended, and I could now enter Radcliffe whenever I pleased. Before I entered college, however, it was thought best that I should study another year under Mr. Keith. It was not, therefore, until the fall of 1900 that my dream of going to college was realized.

I remember my first day at Radcliffe. It was a day full of interest for me. I had looked forward to it for years. A potent force within me, stronger than the persuasion of my friends, stronger even than the pleadings of my heart, had impelled me to try my strength by the standards of those who see and hear. I knew that there were obstacles in the way; but I was eager to overcome them. I had taken to heart the words of the wise Roman who said, "To be banished from Rome is but to live outside of Rome." Debarred from the great highways of knowledge, I was compelled to make the journey across country by unfrequented roads—that was all; and I knew that in college there were many bypaths where I could touch hands with girls who were thinking, loving and struggling like me.

I began my studies with eagerness. Before me I saw a new world opening in beauty and light, and I felt within me the capacity to know all things. In the wonderland of Mind I should be as free as another. Its people, scenery, manners, joys, tragedies should be living, tangible interpreters of the real world. The lecture-halls seemed filled with the spirit of the great and the wise, and I thought the professors were the embodiment of wisdom. If I have since learned differently, I am not going to tell anybody.

But I soon discovered that college was not quite the romantic lyceum I had imagined. Many of the dreams that had delighted my young inexperience became beautifully less and "faded into the light of common day." Gradually I began to find that there were disadvantages in going to college.

The one I felt and still feel most is lack of time. I used to have time to think, to reflect, my mind and I. We would sit together of an evening and listen to the inner melodies of the spirit, which one hears only in leisure moments when the words of some loved poet touch a deep, sweet chord in the soul that until then had been silent. But in college there is no time to commune with one's thoughts. One goes to college to learn, it seems, not to think. When one enters the portals of learning, one leaves the dearest pleasures—solitude, books and imagination—outside with the whispering pines. I suppose I ought to find some comfort in the thought that I am laying up treasures for future enjoyment, but I am improvident enough to prefer present joy to hoarding riches against a rainy day.

My studies the first year were French, German, history, English composition and English literature. In the French course I read some of the works of Corneille, Moliere, Racine, Alfred de Musset and Sainte-Beuve, and in the German those of Goethe and Schiller. I reviewed rapidly the whole period of history from the fall of the Roman Empire to the eighteenth century, and in English literature studied critically Milton's poems and "Areopagitica."

I am frequently asked how I overcome the peculiar conditions under which I work in college. In the classroom I am of course practically alone. The professor is as remote as if he were speaking through a telephone. The lectures are spelled into my hand as rapidly as possible, and much of the individuality of the lecturer is lost to me in the effort to keep in the race. The words rush through my hand like hounds in pursuit of a hare which they often miss. But in this respect I do not think I am much worse off than the girls who take notes. If the mind is occupied with the mechanical process of hearing and putting words on paper at pell-mell speed, I should not think one could pay much attention to the subject under consideration or the manner in which it is presented. I cannot make notes during the lectures, because my hands are busy listening. Usually I jot down what I can remember of them when I get home. I write the exercises, daily themes, criticisms and hour-tests, the mid-year and final examinations, on my typewriter, so that the professors have no difficulty in finding out how little I know. When I began the study of Latin prosody, I devised and explained to my professor a system of signs indicating the different meters and quantities.

I use the Hammond typewriter. I have tried many machines, and I find the Hammond is the best adapted to the peculiar needs of my work. With this machine movable type shuttles can be used, and one can have several shuttles, each with a different set of characters—Greek, French, or mathematical, according to the kind of writing one wishes to do on the typewriter. Without it, I doubt if I could go to college.

Very few of the books required in the various courses are printed for the blind, and I am obliged to have them spelled into my hand. Consequently I need more time to prepare my lessons than other girls. The manual part takes longer, and I have perplexities which they have not. There are days when the close attention I must give to details chafes my spirit, and the thought that I must spend hours reading a few chapters, while in the world without other girls are laughing and singing and dancing, makes me rebellious; but I soon recover my buoyancy and laugh the discontent out of my heart. For, after all, every one who wishes to gain true knowledge must climb the Hill Difficulty alone, and since there is no royal road to the summit, I must zigzag it in my own way. I slip back many times, I fall, I stand still, I run against the edge of hidden obstacles, I lose my temper and find it again and keep it better, I trudge on, I gain a little, I feel encouraged, I get more eager and climb higher and begin to see the widening horizon. Every struggle is a victory. One more effort and I reach the luminous cloud, the blue depths of the sky, the uplands of my desire. I am not always alone, however, in these struggles.

Mr. William Wade and Mr. E. E. Allen, Principal of the Pennsylvania Institution for the Instruction of the Blind, get for me many of the books I need in raised print. Their thoughtfulness has been more of a help and encouragement to me than they can ever know.

Last year, my second year at Radcliffe, I studied English composition, the Bible as English composition, the governments of America and Europe, the Odes of Horace, and Latin comedy. The class in composition was the pleasantest. It was very lively. The lectures were always interesting, vivacious, witty; for the instructor, Mr. Charles Townsend Copeland, more than any one else I have had until this year, brings before you literature in all its original freshness and power. For one short hour you are permitted to drink in the eternal beauty of the old masters without needless interpretation or exposition. You revel in their fine thoughts. You enjoy with all your soul the sweet thunder of the Old Testament, forgetting the existence of Jahweh and Elohim; and you go home feeling that you have had "a glimpse of that perfection in which spirit and form dwell in immortal harmony; truth and beauty bearing a new growth on the ancient stem of time."

This year is the happiest because I am studying subjects that especially interest me, economics, Elizabethan literature, Shakespeare under Professor George L. Kittredge, and the History of Philosophy under Professor Josiah Royce. Through philosophy one enters with sympathy of comprehension into the traditions of remote ages and other modes of thought, which erewhile seemed alien and without reason.

But college is not the universal Athens I thought it was. There one does not meet the great and the wise face to face; one does not even feel their living touch. They are there, it is true; but they seem mummified. We must extract them from the crannied wall of learning and dissect and analyze them before we can be sure that we have a Milton or an Isaiah, and not merely a clever imitation. Many scholars forget, it seems to me, that our enjoyment of the great works of literature depends more upon the depth of our sympathy than upon our understanding. The trouble is that very few of their laborious explanations stick in the memory. The mind drops them as a branch drops its overripe fruit. It is possible to know a flower, root and stem and all, and all the processes of growth, and yet to have no appreciation of the flower fresh bathed in heaven's dew. Again and again I ask impatiently, "Why concern myself with these explanations and hypotheses?" They fly hither and thither in my thought like blind birds beating the air with ineffectual wings. I do not mean to object to a thorough knowledge of the famous works we read. I object only to the interminable comments and bewildering criticisms that teach but one thing: there are as many opinions as there are men. But when a great scholar like Professor Kittredge interprets what the master said, it is "as if new sight were given the blind." He brings back Shakespeare, the poet.

There are, however, times when I long to sweep away half the things I am expected to learn; for the overtaxed mind cannot enjoy the treasure it has secured at the greatest cost. It is impossible, I think, to read in one day four or five different books in different languages and treating of widely different subjects, and not lose sight of the very ends for which one reads. When one reads hurriedly and nervously, having in mind written tests and examinations, one's brain becomes encumbered with a lot of choice bric-a-brac for which there seems to be little use. At the present time my mind is so full of heterogeneous matter that I almost despair of ever being able to put it in order. Whenever I enter the region that was the kingdom of my mind I feel like the proverbial bull in the china shop. A thousand odds and ends of knowledge come crashing about my head like hailstones, and when I try to escape them, theme-goblins and college nixies of all sorts pursue me, until I wish—oh, may I be forgiven the wicked wish!—that I might smash the idols I came to worship.

But the examinations are the chief bugbears of my college life. Although I have faced them many times and cast them down and made them bite the dust, yet they rise again and menace me with pale looks, until like Bob Acres I feel my courage oozing out at my finger ends. The days before these ordeals take place are spent in cramming your mind with mystic formula and indigestible dates—unpalatable diets, until you wish that books and science and you were buried in the depths of the sea.

At last the dreaded hour arrives, and you are a favoured being indeed if you feel prepared, and are able at the right time to call to your standard thoughts that will aid you in that supreme effort. It happens too often that your trumpet call is unheeded. It is most perplexing and exasperating that just at the moment when you need your memory and a nice sense of discrimination, these faculties take to themselves wings and fly away. The facts you have garnered with such infinite trouble invariably fail you at a pinch.

"Give a brief account of Huss and his work." Huss? Who was he and what did he do? The name looks strangely familiar. You ransack your budget of historic facts much as you would hunt for a bit of silk in a rag-bag. You are sure it is somewhere in your mind near the top—you saw it there the other day when you were looking up the beginnings of the Reformation. But where is it now? You fish out all manner of odds and ends of knowledge—revolutions, schisms, massacres, systems of government; but Huss—where is he? You are amazed at all the things you know which are not on the examination paper. In desperation you seize the budget and dump everything out, and there in a corner is your man, serenely brooding on his own private thought, unconscious of the catastrophe which he has brought upon you.

Just then the proctor informs you that the time is up. With a feeling of intense disgust you kick the mass of rubbish into a corner and go home, your head full of revolutionary schemes to abolish the divine right of professors to ask questions without the consent of the questioned.

It comes over me that in the last two or three pages of this chapter I have used figures which will turn the laugh against me. Ah, here they are—the mixed metaphors mocking and strutting about before me, pointing to the bull in the china shop assailed by hailstones and the bugbears with pale looks, an unanalyzed species! Let them mock on. The words describe so exactly the atmosphere of jostling, tumbling ideas I live in that I will wink at them for once, and put on a deliberate air to say that my ideas of college have changed.

While my days at Radcliffe were still in the future, they were encircled with a halo of romance, which they have lost; but in the transition from romantic to actual I have learned many things I should never have known had I not tried the experiment. One of them is the precious science of patience, which teaches us that we should take our education as we would take a walk in the country, leisurely, our minds hospitably open to impressions of every sort. Such knowledge floods the soul unseen with a soundless tidal wave of deepening thought. "Knowledge is power." Rather, knowledge is happiness, because to have knowledge—broad, deep knowledge—is to know true ends from false, and lofty things from low. To know the thoughts and deeds that have marked man's progress is to feel the great heart-throbs of humanity through the centuries; and if one does not feel in these pulsations a heavenward striving, one must indeed be deaf to the harmonies of life.

↣ Chapter XXI ↢

I HAVE thus far sketched the events of my life, but I have not shown how much I have depended on books not only for pleasure and for the wisdom they bring to all who read, but also for that knowledge which comes to others through their eyes and their ears. Indeed, books have meant so much more in my education than in that of others, that I shall go back to the time when I began to read.

I read my first connected story in May, 1887, when I was seven years old, and from that day to this I have devoured everything in the shape of a printed page that has come within the reach of my hungry finger tips. As I have said, I did not study regularly during the early years of my education; nor did I read according to rule.

At first I had only a few books in raised print—"readers" for beginners, a collection of stories for children, and a book about the earth called "Our World." I think that was all; but I read them over and over, until the words were so worn and pressed I could scarcely make them out. Sometimes Miss Sullivan read to me, spelling into my hand little stories and poems that she knew I should understand; but I preferred reading myself to being read to, because I liked to read again and again the things that pleased me.

It was during my first visit to Boston that I really began to read in good earnest. I was permitted to spend a part of each day in the Institution library, and to wander from bookcase to bookcase, and take down whatever book my fingers lighted upon. And read I did, whether I understood one word in ten or two words on a page. The words themselves fascinated me; but I took no conscious account of what I read. My mind must, however, have been very impressionable at that period, for it retained many words and whole sentences, to the meaning of which I had not the faintest clue; and afterward, when I began to talk and write, these words and sentences would flash out quite naturally, so that my friends wondered at the richness of my vocabulary. I must have read parts of many books (in those early days I think I never read any one book through) and a great deal of poetry in this uncomprehending way, until I discovered "Little Lord Fauntleroy," which was the first book of any consequence I read understandingly.

One day my teacher found me in a corner of the library poring over the pages of "The Scarlet Letter." I was then about eight years old. I remember she asked me if I liked little Pearl, and explained some of the words that had puzzled me. Then she told me that she had a beautiful story about a little boy which she was sure I should like better than "The Scarlet Letter." The name of the story was "Little Lord Fauntleroy," and she promised to read it to me the following summer. But we did not begin the story until August; the first few weeks of my stay at the seashore were so full of discoveries and excitement that I forgot the very existence of books. Then my teacher went to visit some friends in Boston, leaving me for a short time.

When she returned almost the first thing we did was to begin the story of "Little Lord Fauntleroy." I recall distinctly the time and place when we read the first chapters of the fascinating child's story. It was a warm afternoon in August. We were sitting together in a hammock which swung from two solemn pines at a short distance from the house. We had hurried through the dish-washing after luncheon, in order that we might have as long an afternoon as possible for the story. As we hastened through the long grass toward the hammock, the grasshoppers swarmed about us and fastened themselves on our clothes, and I remember that my teacher insisted upon picking them all off before we sat down, which seemed to me an unnecessary waste of time. The hammock was covered with pine needles, for it had not been used while my teacher was away. The warm sun shone on the pine trees and drew out all their fragrance. The air was balmy, with a tang of the sea in it. Before we began the story Miss Sullivan explained to me the things that she knew I should not understand, and as we read on she explained the unfamiliar words. At first there were many words I did not know, and the reading was constantly interrupted; but as soon as I thoroughly comprehended the situation, I became too eagerly absorbed in the story to notice mere words, and I am afraid I listened impatiently to the explanations that Miss Sullivan felt to be necessary. When her fingers were too tired to spell another word, I had for the first time a keen sense of my deprivations. I took the book in my hands and tried to feel the letters with an intensity of longing that I can never forget.

Afterward, at my eager request, Mr. Anagnos had this story embossed, and I read it again and again, until I almost knew it by heart; and all through my childhood "Little Lord Fauntleroy" was my sweet and gentle companion. I have given these details at the risk of being tedious, because they are in such vivid contrast with my vague, mutable and confused memories of earlier reading.

From "Little Lord Fauntleroy" I date the beginning of my true interest in books. During the next two years I read many books at my home and on my visits to Boston. I cannot remember what they all were, or in what order I read them; but I know that among them were "Greek Heroes," La Fontaine's "Fables," Hawthorne's "Wonder Book," "Bible Stories," Lamb's "Tales from Shakespeare," "A Child's History of England" by Dickens, "The Arabian Nights," "The Swiss Family Robinson," "The Pilgrim's Progress," "Robinson Crusoe," "Little Women," and "Heidi," a beautiful little story which I afterward read in German. I read them in the intervals between study and play with an ever-deepening sense of pleasure. I did not study nor analyze them—I did not know whether they were well written or not; I never thought about style or authorship. They laid their treasures at my feet, and I accepted them as we accept the sunshine and the love of our friends. I loved "Little Women" because it gave me a sense of kinship with girls and boys who could see and hear.

Circumscribed as my life was in so many ways, I had to look between the covers of books for news of the world that lay outside my own.

I did not care especially for "The Pilgrim's Progress," which I think I did not finish, or for the "Fables." I read La Fontaine's "Fables" first in an English translation, and enjoyed them only after a half-hearted fashion. Later I read the book again in French, and I found that, in spite of the vivid word-pictures, and the wonderful mastery of language, I liked it no better. I do not know why it is, but stories in which animals are made to talk and act like human beings have never appealed to me very strongly. The ludicrous caricatures of the animals occupy my mind to the exclusion of the moral.

Then, again, La Fontaine seldom, if ever, appeals to our highest moral sense. The highest chords he strikes are those of reason and self-love. Through all the fables runs the thought that man's morality springs wholly from self-love, and that if that self-love is directed and restrained by reason, happiness must follow. Now, so far as I can judge, self-love is the root of all evil; but, of course, I may be wrong, for La Fontaine had greater opportunities of observing men than I am likely ever to have. I do not object so much to the cynical and satirical fables as to those in which momentous truths are taught by monkeys and foxes.

But I love "The Jungle Book" and "Wild Animals I Have Known." I feel a genuine interest in the animals themselves, because they are real animals and not caricatures of men. One sympathizes with their loves and hatreds, laughs over their comedies, and weeps over their tragedies. And if they point a moral, it is so subtle that we are not conscious of it.

My mind opened naturally and joyously to a conception of antiquity. Greece, ancient Greece, exercised a mysterious fascination over me. In my fancy the pagan gods and goddesses still walked on earth and talked face to face with men, and in my heart I secretly built shrines to those I loved best. I knew and loved the whole tribe of nymphs and heroes and demigods—no, not quite all, for the cruelty and greed of Medea and Jason were too monstrous to be forgiven, and I used to wonder why the gods permitted them to do wrong and then punished them for their wickedness. And the mystery is still unsolved. I often wonder how

> *God can dumbness keep*
> *While Sin creeps grinning through His house of Time.*

It was the Iliad that made Greece my paradise. I was familiar with the story of Troy before I read it in the original, and consequently I had little difficulty in making the Greek words surrender their treasures after I had passed the borderland of grammar. Great poetry, whether written in Greek or in English, needs no other interpreter than a responsive heart. Would that the host of those who make the great works of the poets odious by their analysis, impositions and laborious comments might learn this simple truth! It is not necessary that one should be able to define every word and give it its principal parts and its grammatical position in the sentence in order to understand and appreciate a fine poem. I know my learned professors have found greater riches in the Iliad than I shall ever find; but I am not avaricious. I am content that others should be wiser than I. But with all their wide and comprehensive knowledge, they cannot measure their enjoyment of that splendid epic, nor can I. When I read the finest passages of the Iliad, I am conscious of a soul-sense that lifts me above the narrow, cramping circumstances of my life. My physical limitations are forgotten—my world lies upward, the length and the breadth and the sweep of the heavens are mine!

My admiration for the Aeneid is not so great, but it is none the less real. I read it as much as possible without the help of notes or dictionary, and I always like to translate the episodes that please me especially. The word-painting of Virgil is wonderful sometimes; but his gods and men move through the scenes of passion and strife and pity and love like the graceful figures in an Elizabethan mask, whereas in the Iliad they give three leaps and go on singing. Virgil is serene and lovely like a marble Apollo in the moonlight; Homer is a beautiful, animated youth in the full sunlight with the wind in his hair.

How easy it is to fly on paper wings! From "Greek Heroes" to the Iliad was no day's journey, nor was it altogether pleasant. One could have traveled round the word many times while I trudged my weary way through the labyrinthine mazes of grammars and dictionaries, or fell into those dreadful pitfalls called examinations, set by schools and colleges for the confusion of those who seek after knowledge. I suppose this sort of Pilgrim's Progress was justified by the end; but it seemed interminable to me, in spite of the pleasant surprises that met me now and then at a turn in the road.

I began to read the Bible long before I could understand it. Now it seems strange to me that there should have been a time when my spirit was deaf to its wondrous harmonies; but I remember well a rainy Sunday morning when, having nothing else to do, I begged my cousin to read me a story out of the Bible. Although she did not think I should understand, she began to spell into my hand the story of Joseph and his brothers. Somehow it failed to interest me. The unusual language and repetition made the story seem unreal and far away in the land of Canaan, and I fell asleep and wandered off to the land of Nod, before the brothers came with the coat of many colours unto the tent of Jacob and told their wicked lie! I cannot understand why the stories of the Greeks should have been so full of charm for me, and those of the Bible so devoid of interest, unless it was that I had made the acquaintance of several Greeks in Boston and been inspired by their enthusiasm for the stories of their country; whereas I had not met a single Hebrew or Egyptian, and therefore concluded that they were nothing more than barbarians, and the stories about them were probably all made up, which hypothesis explained the repetitions and the queer names. Curiously enough, it never occurred to me to call Greek patronymics "queer."

But how shall I speak of the glories I have since discovered in the Bible? For years I have read it with an ever-broadening sense of joy and inspiration; and I love it as I love no other book. Still there is much in the Bible against which every instinct of my being rebels, so much that I regret the necessity which has compelled me to read it through from beginning to end. I do not think that the knowledge which I have gained of its history and sources compensates me for the unpleasant details it has forced upon my attention. For my part, I wish, with Mr. Howells, that the literature of the past might be purged of all that is ugly and barbarous in it, although I should object as much as any one to having these great works weakened or falsified.

There is something impressive, awful, in the simplicity and terrible directness of the book of Esther. Could there be anything more dramatic than the scene in which Esther stands before her wicked lord? She knows her life is in his hands; there is no one to protect her from his wrath. Yet, conquering her woman's fear, she approaches him, animated by the noblest patriotism, having but one thought: "If I perish, I perish; but if I live, my people shall live."

The story of Ruth, too—how Oriental it is! Yet how different is the life of these simple country folks from that of the Persian capital! Ruth is so loyal and gentle-hearted, we cannot help loving her, as she stands with the reapers amid the waving corn. Her beautiful, unselfish spirit shines out like a bright star in the night of a dark and cruel age. Love like Ruth's, love which can rise above conflicting creeds and deep-seated racial prejudices, is hard to find in all the world.

The Bible gives me a deep, comforting sense that "things seen are temporal, and things unseen are eternal."

I do not remember a time since I have been capable of loving books that I have not loved Shakespeare. I cannot tell exactly when I began Lamb's "Tales from Shakespeare"; but I know that I read them at first with a child's understanding and a child's wonder. "Macbeth" seems to have impressed me most. One reading was sufficient to stamp every detail of the story upon my memory forever. For a long time the ghosts and witches pursued me even into Dreamland. I could see, absolutely see, the dagger and Lady Macbeth's little white hand—the dreadful stain was as real to me as to the grief-stricken queen.

I read "King Lear" soon after "Macbeth," and I shall never forget the feeling of horror when I came to the scene in which Gloster's eyes are put out. Anger seized me, my fingers refused to move, I sat rigid for one long moment, the blood throbbing in my temples, and all the hatred that a child can feel concentrated in my heart.

I must have made the acquaintance of Shylock and Satan about the same time, for the two characters were long associated in my mind. I remember that I was sorry for them. I felt vaguely that they could not be good even if they wished to, because no one seemed willing to help them or to give them a fair chance. Even now I cannot find it in my heart to condemn them utterly. There are moments when I feel that the Shylocks, the Judases, and even the Devil, are broken spokes in the great wheel of good which shall in due time be made whole.

It seems strange that my first reading of Shakespeare should have left me so many unpleasant memories. The bright, gentle, fanciful plays— the ones I like best now—appear not to have impressed me at first, perhaps because they reflected the habitual sunshine and gaiety of a child's life. But "there is nothing more capricious than the memory of a child: what it will hold, and what it will lose."

I have since read Shakespeare's plays many times and know parts of them by heart, but I cannot tell which of them I like best. My delight in them is as varied as my moods. The little songs and the sonnets have a meaning for me as fresh and wonderful as the dramas. But, with all my love for Shakespeare, it is often weary work to read all the meanings into his lines which critics and commentators have given them. I used to try to remember their interpretations, but they discouraged and vexed me; so I made a secret compact with myself not to try any more. This compact I have only just broken in my study of Shakespeare under Professor Kittredge. I know there are many things in Shakespeare, and in the world, that I do not understand; and I am glad to see veil after veil lift gradually, revealing new realms of thought and beauty.

Next to poetry I love history. I have read every historical work that I have been able to lay my hands on, from a catalogue of dry facts and dryer dates to Green's impartial, picturesque "History of the English People"; from Freeman's "History of Europe" to Emerton's "Middle Ages." The first book that gave me any real sense of the value of history was Swinton's "World History," which I received on my thirteenth birthday. Though I believe it is no longer considered valid, yet I have kept it ever since as one of my treasures. From it I learned how the races of men spread from land to land and built great cities, how a few great rulers, earthly Titans, put everything under their feet, and with a decisive word opened the gates of happiness for millions and closed them upon millions more: how different nations pioneered in art and knowledge and broke ground for the mightier growths of coming ages; how civilization underwent as it were, the holocaust of a degenerate age, and rose again, like the Phoenix, among the nobler sons of the North; and how by liberty, tolerance and education the great and the wise have opened the way for the salvation of the whole world.

In my college reading I have become somewhat familiar with French and German literature. The German puts strength before beauty, and truth before convention, both in life and in literature. There is a vehement, sledge-hammer vigour about everything that he does. When he speaks, it is not to impress others, but because his heart would burst if he did not find an outlet for the thoughts that burn in his soul.

Then, too, there is in German literature a fine reserve which I like; but its chief glory is the recognition I find in it of the redeeming potency of woman's self-sacrificing love. This thought pervades all German literature and is mystically expressed in Goethe's "Faust":

> *All things transitory*
> *But as symbols are sent.*
> *Earth's insufficiency*
> *Here grows to event.*
> *The indescribable*
> *Here it is done.*
> *The Woman Soul leads us upward and on!*

Of all the French writers that I have read, I like Moliere and Racine best. There are fine things in Balzac and passages in Merimee which strike one like a keen blast of sea air. Alfred de Musset is impossible! I admire Victor Hugo—I appreciate his genius, his brilliancy, his romanticism; though he is not one of my literary passions. But Hugo and Goethe and Schiller and all great poets of all great nations are interpreters of eternal things, and my spirit reverently follows them into the regions where Beauty and Truth and Goodness are one.

I am afraid I have written too much about my book-friends, and yet I have mentioned only the authors I love most; and from this fact one might easily suppose that my circle of friends was very limited and undemocratic, which would be a very wrong impression. I like many writers for many reasons—Carlyle for his ruggedness and scorn of shams; Wordsworth, who teaches the oneness of man and nature; I find an exquisite pleasure in the oddities and surprises of Hood, in Herrick's quaintness and the palpable scent of lily and rose in his verses; I like Whittier for his enthusiasms and moral rectitude. I knew him, and the gentle remembrance of our friendship doubles the pleasure I have in reading his poems. I love Mark Twain—who does not? The gods, too, loved him and put into his heart all manner of wisdom; then, fearing lest he should become a pessimist, they spanned his mind with a rainbow of love and faith. I like Scott for his freshness, dash and large honesty. I love all writers whose minds, like Lowell's, bubble up in the sunshine of optimism—fountains of joy and good will, with occasionally a splash of anger and here and there a healing spray of sympathy and pity.

In a word, literature is my Utopia. Here I am not disfranchised. No barrier of the senses shuts me out from the sweet, gracious discourse of my book-friends. They talk to me without embarrassment or awkwardness. The things I have learned and the things I have been taught seem of ridiculously little importance compared with their "large loves and heavenly charities."

Chapter XXII

I TRUST that my readers have not concluded from the preceding chapter on books that reading is my only pleasure; my pleasures and amusements are many and varied.

More than once in the course of my story I have referred to my love of the country and out-of-door sports. When I was quite a little girl, I learned to row and swim, and during the summer, when I am at Wrentham, Massachusetts, I almost live in my boat. Nothing gives me greater pleasure than to take my friends out rowing when they visit me. Of course, I cannot guide the boat very well. Some one usually sits in the stern and manages the rudder while I row. Sometimes, however, I go rowing without the rudder. It is fun to try to steer by the scent of watergrasses and lilies, and of bushes that grow on the shore. I use oars with leather bands, which keep them in position in the oarlocks, and I know by the resistance of the water when the oars are evenly poised. In the same manner I can also tell when I am pulling against the current. I like to contend with wind and wave. What is more exhilarating than to make your staunch little boat, obedient to your will and muscle, go skimming lightly over glistening, tilting waves, and to feel the steady, imperious surge of the water!

I also enjoy canoeing, and I suppose you will smile when I say that I especially like it on moonlight nights. I cannot, it is true, see the moon climb up the sky behind the pines and steal softly across the heavens, making a shining path for us to follow; but I know she is there, and as I lie back among the pillows and put my hand in the water, I fancy that I feel the shimmer of her garments as she passes. Sometimes a daring little fish slips between my fingers, and often a pond-lily presses shyly against my hand. Frequently, as we emerge from the shelter of a cove or inlet, I am suddenly conscious of the spaciousness of the air about me. A luminous warmth seems to enfold me. Whether it comes from the trees which have been heated by the sun, or from the water, I can never discover. I have had the same strange sensation even in the heart of the city. I have felt it on cold, stormy days and at night. It is like the kiss of warm lips on my face.

My favourite amusement is sailing. In the summer of 1901 I visited Nova Scotia, and had opportunities such as I had not enjoyed before to make the acquaintance of the ocean. After spending a few days in Evangeline's country, about which Longfellow's beautiful poem has woven a spell of enchantment, Miss Sullivan and I went to Halifax, where we remained the greater part of the summer. The harbour was our joy, our paradise. What glorious sails we had to Bedford Basin, to McNabb's Island, to York Redoubt, and to the Northwest Arm! And at night what soothing, wondrous hours we spent in the shadow of the great, silent men-of-war. Oh, it was all so interesting, so beautiful! The memory of it is a joy forever.

One day we had a thrilling experience. There was a regatta in the Northwest Arm, in which the boats from the different warships were engaged. We went in a sail-boat along with many others to watch the races. Hundreds of little sail-boats swung to and fro close by, and the sea was calm. When the races were over, and we turned our faces homeward, one of the party noticed a black cloud drifting in from the sea, which grew and spread and thickened until it covered the whole sky. The wind rose, and the waves chopped angrily at unseen barriers. Our little boat confronted the gale fearlessly; with sails spread and ropes taut, she seemed to sit upon the wind. Now she swirled in the billows, now she spring upward on a gigantic wave, only to be driven down with angry howl and hiss. Down came the mainsail. Tacking and jibbing, we wrestled with opposing winds that drove us from side to side with impetuous fury. Our hearts beat fast, and our hands trembled with excitement, not fear, for we had the hearts of vikings, and we knew that our skipper was master of the situation. He had steered through many a storm with firm hand and sea-wise eye. As they passed us, the large craft and the gunboats in the harbour saluted and the seamen shouted applause for the master of the only little sail-boat that ventured out into the storm. At last, cold, hungry and weary, we reached our pier.

Last summer I spent in one of the loveliest nooks of one of the most charming villages in New England. Wrentham, Massachusetts, is associated with nearly all of my joys and sorrows. For many years Red Farm, by King Philip's Pond, the home of Mr. J. E. Chamberlin and his family, was my home. I remember with deepest gratitude the kindness of these dear friends and the happy days I spent with them. The sweet companionship of their children meant much to me. I joined in all their sports and rambles through the woods and frolics in the water. The prattle of the little ones and their pleasure in the stories I told them of elf and gnome, of hero and wily bear, are pleasant things to remember. Mr. Chamberlin initiated me into the mysteries of tree and wild-flower, until with the little ear of love I heard the flow of sap in the oak, and saw the sun glint from leaf to leaf.

> *Thus it is that*
> *Even as the roots, shut in the darksome earth,*
> *Share in the tree-top's joyance, and conceive*
> *Of sunshine and wide air and winged things,*
> *By sympathy of nature, so do*
> *I gave evidence of things unseen.*

It seems to me that there is in each of us a capacity to comprehend the impressions and emotions which have been experienced by mankind from the beginning. Each individual has a subconscious memory of the green earth and murmuring waters, and blindness and deafness cannot rob him of this gift from past generations. This inherited capacity is a sort of sixth sense—a soul-sense which sees, hears, feels, all in one.

I have many tree friends in Wrentham. One of them, a splendid oak, is the special pride of my heart. I take all my other friends to see this king-tree. It stands on a bluff overlooking King Philip's Pond, and those who are wise in tree lore say it must have stood there eight hundred or a thousand years. There is a tradition that under this tree King Philip, the heroic Indian chief, gazed his last on earth and sky.

I had another tree friend, gentle and more approachable than the great oak—a linden that grew in the dooryard at Red Farm. One afternoon, during a terrible thunderstorm, I felt a tremendous crash against the side of the house and knew, even before they told me, that the linden had fallen. We went out to see the hero that had withstood so many tempests, and it wrung my heart to see him prostrate who had mightily striven and was now mightily fallen.

But I must not forget that I was going to write about last summer in particular. As soon as my examinations were over, Miss Sullivan and I hastened to this green nook, where we have a little cottage on one of the three lakes for which Wrentham is famous. Here the long, sunny days were mine, and all thoughts of work and college and the noisy city were thrust into the background. In Wrentham we caught echoes of what was happening in the world—war, alliance, social conflict. We heard of the cruel, unnecessary fighting in the far-away Pacific, and learned of the struggles going on between capital and labour. We knew that beyond the border of our Eden men were making history by the sweat of their brows when they might better make a holiday. But we little heeded these things. These things would pass away; here were lakes and woods and broad daisy-starred fields and sweet-breathed meadows, and they shall endure forever.

People who think that all sensations reach us through the eye and the ear have expressed surprise that I should notice any difference, except possibly the absence of pavements, between walking in city streets and in country roads. They forget that my whole body is alive to the conditions about me. The rumble and roar of the city smite the nerves of my face, and I feel the ceaseless tramp of an unseen multitude, and the dissonant tumult frets my spirit. The grinding of heavy wagons on hard pavements and the monotonous clangour of machinery are all the more torturing to the nerves if one's attention is not diverted by the panorama that is always present in the noisy streets to people who can see.

In the country one sees only Nature's fair works, and one's soul is not saddened by the cruel struggle for mere existence that goes on in the crowded city. Several times I have visited the narrow, dirty streets where the poor live, and I grow hot and indignant to think that good people should be content to live in fine houses and become strong and beautiful, while others are condemned to live in hideous, sunless tenements and grow ugly, withered and cringing. The children who crowd these grimy alleys, half-clad and underfed, shrink away from your outstretched hand as if from a blow. Dear little creatures, they crouch in my heart and haunt me with a constant sense of pain. There are men and women, too, all gnarled and bent out of shape. I have felt their hard, rough hands and realized what an endless struggle their existence must be—no more than a series of scrimmages, thwarted attempts to do something. Their life seems an immense disparity between effort and opportunity. The sun and the air are God's free gifts to all we say, but are they so? In yonder city's dingy alleys the sun shines not, and the air is foul. Oh, man, how dost thou forget and obstruct thy brother man, and say, "Give us this day our daily bread," when he has none! Oh, would that men would leave the city, its splendour and its tumult and its gold, and return to wood and field and simple, honest living! Then would their children grow stately as noble trees, and their thoughts sweet and pure as wayside flowers. It is impossible not to think of all this when I return to the country after a year of work in town.

What a joy it is to feel the soft, springy earth under my feet once more, to follow grassy roads that lead to ferny brooks where I can bathe my fingers in a cataract of rippling notes, or to clamber over a stone wall into green fields that tumble and roll and climb in riotous gladness!

Next to a leisurely walk I enjoy a "spin" on my tandem bicycle. It is splendid to feel the wind blowing in my face and the springy motion of my iron steed. The rapid rush through the air gives me a delicious sense of strength and buoyancy, and the exercise makes my pulses dance and my heart sing.

Whenever it is possible, my dog accompanies me on a walk or ride or sail. I have had many dog friends—huge mastiffs, soft-eyed spaniels, wood-wise setters and honest, homely bull terriers. At present the lord of my affections is one of these bull terriers. He has a long pedigree, a crooked tail and the drollest "phiz" in dogdom. My dog friends seem to understand my limitations, and always keep close beside me when I am alone. I love their affectionate ways and the eloquent wag of their tails.

When a rainy day keeps me indoors, I amuse myself after the manner of other girls. I like to knit and crochet; I read in the happy-go-lucky way I love, here and there a line; or perhaps I play a game or two of checkers or chess with a friend. I have a special board on which I play these games. The squares are cut out, so that the men stand in them firmly. The black checkers are flat and the white ones curved on top. Each checker has a hole in the middle in which a brass knob can be placed to distinguish the king from the commons. The chessmen are of two sizes, the white larger than the black, so that I have no trouble in following my opponent's maneuvers by moving my hands lightly over the board after a play. The jar made by shifting the men from one hole to another tells me when it is my turn.

If I happen to be all alone and in an idle mood, I play a game of solitaire, of which I am very fond. I use playing cards marked in the upper right-hand corner with braille symbols which indicate the value of the card.

If there are children around, nothing pleases me so much as to frolic with them. I find even the smallest child excellent company, and I am glad to say that children usually like me. They lead me about and show me the things they are interested in. Of course the little ones cannot spell on their fingers; but I manage to read their lips. If I do not succeed they resort to dumb show. Sometimes I make a mistake and do the wrong thing. A burst of childish laughter greets my blunder, and the pantomime begins all over again. I often tell them stories or teach them a game, and the winged hours depart and leave us good and happy.

Museums and art stores are also sources of pleasure and inspiration. Doubtless it will seem strange to many that the hand unaided by sight can feel action, sentiment, beauty in the cold marble; and yet it is true that I derive genuine pleasure from touching great works of art. As my finger tips trace line and curve, they discover the thought and emotion which the artist has portrayed. I can feel in the faces of gods and heroes hate, courage and love, just as I can detect them in living faces I am permitted to touch. I feel in Diana's posture the grace and freedom of the forest and the spirit that tames the mountain lion and subdues the fiercest passions. My soul delights in the repose and gracious curves of the Venus; and in Barre's bronzes the secrets of the jungle are revealed to me.

A medallion of Homer hangs on the wall of my study, conveniently low, so that I can easily reach it and touch the beautiful, sad face with loving reverence. How well I know each line in that majestic brow—tracks of life and bitter evidences of struggle and sorrow; those sightless eyes seeking, even in the cold plaster, for the light and the blue skies of his beloved Hellas, but seeking in vain; that beautiful mouth, firm and true and tender. It is the face of a poet, and of a man acquainted with sorrow. Ah, how well I understand his deprivation—the perpetual night in which he dwelt—

> *O dark, dark, amid the blaze of noon,*
> *Irrecoverably dark, total eclipse*
> *Without all hope of day!*

In imagination I can hear Homer singing, as with unsteady, hesitating steps he gropes his way from camp to camp—singing of life, of love, of war, of the splendid achievements of a noble race. It was a wonderful, glorious song, and it won the blind poet an immortal crown, the admiration of all ages.

I sometimes wonder if the hand is not more sensitive to the beauties of sculpture than the eye. I should think the wonderful rhythmical flow of lines and curves could be more subtly felt than seen. Be this as it may, I know that I can feel the heart-throbs of the ancient Greeks in their marble gods and goddesses.

Another pleasure, which comes more rarely than the others, is going to the theatre. I enjoy having a play described to me while it is being acted on the stage far more than reading it, because then it seems as if I were living in the midst of stirring events. It has been my privilege to meet a few great actors and actresses who have the power of so bewitching you that you forget time and place and live again in the romantic past. I have been permitted to touch the face and costume of Miss Ellen Terry as she impersonated our ideal of a queen; and there was about her that divinity that hedges sublimest woe. Beside her stood Sir Henry Irving, wearing the symbols of kingship; and there was majesty of intellect in his every gesture and attitude and the royalty that subdues and overcomes in every line of his sensitive face. In the king's face, which he wore as a mask, there was a remoteness and inaccessibility of grief which I shall never forget.

I also know Mr. Jefferson. I am proud to count him among my friends. I go to see him whenever I happen to be where he is acting. The first time I saw him act was while at school in New York. He played "Rip Van Winkle." I had often read the story, but I had never felt the charm of Rip's slow, quaint, kind ways as I did in the play. Mr. Jefferson's, beautiful, pathetic representation quite carried me away with delight. I have a picture of old Rip in my fingers which they will never lose. After the play Miss Sullivan took me to see him behind the scenes, and I felt of his curious garb and his flowing hair and beard. Mr. Jefferson let me touch his face so that I could imagine how he looked on waking from that strange sleep of twenty years, and he showed me how poor old Rip staggered to his feet.

I have also seen him in "The Rivals." Once while I was calling on him in Boston he acted the most striking parts of "The Rivals" for me. The reception-room where we sat served for a stage. He and his son seated themselves at the big table, and Bob Acres wrote his challenge. I followed all his movements with my hands, and caught the drollery of his blunders and gestures in a way that would have been impossible had it all been spelled to me. Then they rose to fight the duel, and I followed the swift thrusts and parries of the swords and the waverings of poor Bob as his courage oozed out at his finger ends. Then the great actor gave his coat a hitch and his mouth a twitch, and in an instant I was in the village of Falling Water and felt Schneider's shaggy head against my knee. Mr. Jefferson recited the best dialogues of "Rip Van Winkle," in which the tear came close upon the smile. He asked me to indicate as far as I could the gestures and action that should go with the lines. Of course, I have no sense whatever of dramatic action, and could make only random guesses;

but with masterful art he suited the action to the word. The sigh of Rip as he murmurs, "Is a man so soon forgotten when he is gone?" the dismay with which he searches for dog and gun after his long sleep, and his comical irresolution over signing the contract with Derrick—all these seem to be right out of life itself; that is, the ideal life, where things happen as we think they should.

I remember well the first time I went to the theatre. It was twelve years ago. Elsie Leslie, the little actress, was in Boston, and Miss Sullivan took me to see her in "The Prince and the Pauper." I shall never forget the ripple of alternating joy and woe that ran through that beautiful little play, or the wonderful child who acted it. After the play I was permitted to go behind the scenes and meet her in her royal costume. It would have been hard to find a lovelier or more lovable child than Elsie, as she stood with a cloud of golden hair floating over her shoulders, smiling brightly, showing no signs of shyness or fatigue, though she had been playing to an immense audience. I was only just learning to speak, and had previously repeated her name until I could say it perfectly. Imagine my delight when she understood the few words I spoke to her and without hesitation stretched her hand to greet me.

Is it not true, then, that my life with all its limitations touches at many points the life of the World Beautiful? Everything has its wonders, even darkness and silence, and I learn, whatever state I may be in, therein to be content.

Sometimes, it is true, a sense of isolation enfolds me like a cold mist as I sit alone and wait at life's shut gate. Beyond there is light, and music, and sweet companionship; but I may not enter. Fate, silent, pitiless, bars the way. Fain would I question his imperious decree, for my heart is still undisciplined and passionate; but my tongue will not utter the bitter, futile words that rise to my lips, and they fall back into my heart like unshed tears. Silence sits immense upon my soul. Then comes hope with a smile and whispers, "There is joy in self-forgetfulness." So I try to make the light in others' eyes my sun, the music in others' ears my symphony, the smile on others' lips my happiness.

Chapter XXIII

WOULD THAT I could enrich this sketch with the names of all those who have ministered to my happiness! Some of them would be found written in our literature and dear to the hearts of many, while others would be wholly unknown to most of my readers. But their influence, though it escapes fame, shall live immortal in the lives that have been sweetened and ennobled by it. Those are red-letter days in our lives when we meet people who thrill us like a fine poem, people whose handshake is brimful of unspoken sympathy, and whose sweet, rich natures impart to our eager, impatient spirits a wonderful restfulness which, in its essence, is divine. The perplexities, irritations and worries that have absorbed us pass like unpleasant dreams, and we wake to see with new eyes and hear with new ears the beauty and harmony of God's real world. The solemn nothings that fill our everyday life blossom suddenly into bright possibilities. In a word, while such friends are near us we feel that all is well. Perhaps we never saw them before, and they may never cross our life's path again; but the influence of their calm, mellow natures is a libation poured upon our discontent, and we feel its healing touch, as the ocean feels the mountain stream freshening its brine.

I have often been asked, "Do not people bore you?" I do not understand quite what that means. I suppose the calls of the stupid and curious, especially of newspaper reporters, are always inopportune. I also dislike people who try to talk down to my understanding. They are like people who when walking with you try to shorten their steps to suit yours; the hypocrisy in both cases is equally exasperating.

The hands of those I meet are dumbly eloquent to me. The touch of some hands is an impertinence. I have met people so empty of joy, that when I clasped their frosty finger tips, it seemed as if I were shaking hands with a northeast storm. Others there are whose hands have sunbeams in them, so that their grasp warms my heart. It may be only the clinging touch of a child's hand; but there is as much potential sunshine in it for me as there is in a loving glance for others. A hearty handshake or a friendly letter gives me genuine pleasure.

I have many far-off friends whom I have never seen. Indeed they are so many that I have often been unable to reply to their letters; but I wish to say here that I am always grateful for their kind words, however insufficiently I acknowledge them.

I count it one of the sweetest privileges of my life to have known and conversed with many men of genius. Only those who knew Bishop Brooks can appreciate the joy his friendship was to those who possessed it. As a child I loved to sit on his knee and clasp his great hand with one of mine, while Miss Sullivan spelled into the other his beautiful words about God and the spiritual world. I heard him with a child's wonder and delight. My spirit could not reach up to his, but he gave me a real sense of joy in life, and I never left him without carrying away a fine thought that grew in beauty and depth of meaning as I grew. Once, when I was puzzled to know why there were so many religions, he said: "There is one universal religion, Helen—the religion of love. Love your Heavenly Father with your whole heart and soul, love every child of God as much as ever you can, and remember that the possibilities of good are greater than the possibilities of evil; and you have the key to Heaven." And his life was a happy illustration of this great truth. In his noble soul love and widest knowledge were blended with faith that had become insight. He saw

> *God in all that liberates and lifts,*
> *In all that humbles, sweetens and consoles.*

Bishop Brooks taught me no special creed or dogma; but he impressed upon my mind two great ideas—the fatherhood of God and the brotherhood of man, and made me feel that these truths underlie all creeds and forms of worship. God is love, God is our Father, we are His children; therefore the darkest clouds will break and though right be worsted, wrong shall not triumph.

I am too happy in this world to think much about the future, except to remember that I have cherished friends awaiting me there in God's beautiful Somewhere. In spite of the lapse of years, they seem so close to me that I should not think it strange if at any moment they should clasp my hand and speak words of endearment as they used to before they went away.

Since Bishop Brooks died I have read the Bible through; also some philosophical works on religion, among them Swedenborg's "Heaven and Hell" and Drummond's "Ascent of Man," and I have found no creed or system more soul-satisfying than Bishop Brooks's creed of love. I knew Mr. Henry Drummond, and the memory of his strong, warm hand-clasp is like a benediction. He was the most sympathetic of companions. He knew so much and was so genial that it was impossible to feel dull in his presence.

I remember well the first time I saw Dr. Oliver Wendell Holmes. He had invited Miss Sullivan and me to call on him one Sunday afternoon. It was early in the spring, just after I had learned to speak. We were shown at once to his library where we found him seated in a big armchair by an open fire which glowed and crackled on the hearth, thinking, he said, of other days.

"And listening to the murmur of the River Charles," I suggested.

"Yes," he replied, "the Charles has many dear associations for me." There was an odour of print and leather in the room which told me that it was full of books, and I stretched out my hand instinctively to find them. My fingers lighted upon a beautiful volume of Tennyson's poems, and when Miss Sullivan told me what it was I began to recite:

Break, break, break
On thy cold gray stones, O sea!

But I stopped suddenly. I felt tears on my hand. I had made my beloved poet weep, and I was greatly distressed. He made me sit in his armchair, while he brought different interesting things for me to examine, and at his request I recited "The Chambered Nautilus," which was then my favorite poem. After that I saw Dr. Holmes many times and learned to love the man as well as the poet.

One beautiful summer day, not long after my meeting with Dr. Holmes, Miss Sullivan and I visited Whittier in his quiet home on the Merrimac. His gentle courtesy and quaint speech won my heart. He had a book of his poems in raised print from which I read "In School Days." He was delighted that I could pronounce the words so well, and said that he had no difficulty in understanding me. Then I asked many questions about the poem, and read his answers by placing my fingers on his lips. He said he was the little boy in the poem, and that the girl's name was Sally, and more which I have forgotten. I also recited "Laus Deo," and as I spoke the concluding verses, he placed in my hands a statue of a slave from whose crouching figure the fetters were falling, even as they fell from Peter's limbs when the angel led him forth out of prison. Afterward we went into his study, and he wrote his autograph for my teacher ["With great admiration of thy noble work in releasing from bondage the mind of thy dear pupil, I am truly thy friend. john J. Whittier."] and expressed his admiration of her work, saying to me, "She is thy spiritual liberator." Then he led me to the gate and kissed me tenderly on my forehead. I promised to visit him again the following summer, but he died before the promise was fulfilled.

Dr. Edward Everett Hale is one of my very oldest friends. I have known him since I was eight, and my love for him has increased with my years. His wise, tender sympathy has been the support of Miss Sullivan and me in times of trial and sorrow, and his strong hand has helped us over many rough places; and what he has done for us he has done for thousands of those who have difficult tasks to accomplish. He has filled the old skins of dogma with the new wine of love, and shown men what it is to believe, live and be free. What he has taught we have seen beautifully expressed in his own life—love of country, kindness to the least of his brethren, and a sincere desire to live upward and onward. He has been a prophet and an inspirer of men, and a mighty doer of the Word, the friend of all his race—God bless him!

I have already written of my first meeting with Dr. Alexander Graham Bell. Since then I have spent many happy days with him at

Washington and at his beautiful home in the heart of Cape Breton Island, near Baddeck, the village made famous by Charles Dudley Warner's book. Here in Dr. Bell's laboratory, or in the fields on the shore of the great Bras d'Or, I have spent many delightful hours listening to what he had to tell me about his experiments, and helping him fly kites by means of which he expects to discover the laws that shall govern the future air-ship. Dr. Bell is proficient in many fields of science, and has the art of making every subject he touches interesting, even the most abstruse theories. He makes you feel that if you only had a little more time, you, too, might be an inventor. He has a humorous and poetic side, too. His dominating passion is his love for children. He is never quite so happy as when he has a little deaf child in his arms. His labours in behalf of the deaf will live on and bless generations of children yet to come; and we love him alike for what he himself has achieved and for what he has evoked from others.

During the two years I spent in New York I had many opportunities to talk with distinguished people whose names I had often heard, but whom I had never expected to meet. Most of them I met first in the house of my good friend, Mr. Laurence Hutton. It was a great privilege to visit him and dear Mrs. Hutton in their lovely home, and see their library and read the beautiful sentiments and bright thoughts gifted friends had written for them. It has been truly said that Mr. Hutton has the faculty of bringing out in every one the best thoughts and kindest sentiments. One does not need to read "A Boy I Knew" to understand him—the most generous, sweet-natured boy I ever knew, a good friend in all sorts of weather, who traces the footprints of love in the life of dogs as well as in that of his fellowmen.

Mrs. Hutton is a true and tried friend. Much that I hold sweetest, much that I hold most precious, I owe to her. She has oftenest advised and helped me in my progress through college. When I find my work particularly difficult and discouraging, she writes me letters that make me feel glad and brave; for she is one of those from whom we learn that one painful duty fulfilled makes the next plainer and easier.

Mr. Hutton introduced me to many of his literary friends, greatest of whom are Mr. William Dean Howells and Mark Twain. I also met Mr. Richard Watson Gilder and Mr. Edmund Clarence Stedman. I also knew Mr. Charles Dudley Warner, the most delightful of story-tellers and the most beloved friend, whose sympathy was so broad that it may be truly said of him, he loved all living things and his neighbour as himself. Once Mr. Warner brought to see me the dear poet of the woodlands—Mr. John Burroughs. They were all gentle and sympathetic and I felt the charm of their manner as much as I had felt the brilliancy of their essays and poems. I could not keep pace with all these literary folk as they glanced from subject to subject and entered into deep dispute, or made conversation sparkle with epigrams and happy witticisms. I was like little Ascanius, who followed with unequal steps the heroic strides of Aeneas on his march toward mighty destinies. But they spoke many gracious words to me. Mr. Gilder told me about his moonlight journeys across the vast desert to the Pyramids, and in a letter he wrote me he made his mark under his signature deep in the paper so that I could feel it. This reminds me that Dr. Hale used to give a personal touch to his letters to me by pricking his signature in braille. I read from Mark Twain's lips one or two of his good stories. He has his own way of thinking, saying and doing everything. I feel the twinkle of his eye in his handshake. Even while he utters his cynical wisdom in an indescribably droll voice, he makes you feel that his heart is a tender Iliad of human sympathy.

There are a host of other interesting people I met in New York: Mrs. Mary Mapes Dodge, the beloved editor of St. Nicholas, and Mrs. Riggs (Kate Douglas Wiggin), the sweet author of "Patsy." I received from them gifts that have the gentle concurrence of the heart, books containing their own thoughts, soul-illumined letters, and photographs that I love to have described again and again. But there is not space to mention all my friends, and indeed there are things about them hidden behind the wings of cherubim, things too sacred to set forth in cold print. It is with hesitancy that I have spoken even of Mrs. Laurence Hutton.

I shall mention only two other friends. One is Mrs. William Thaw, of Pittsburgh, whom I have often visited in her home, Lyndhurst. She is always doing something to make some one happy, and her generosity and wise counsel have never failed my teacher and me in all the years we have known her.

To the other friend I am also deeply indebted. He is well known for the powerful hand with which he guides vast enterprises, and his wonderful abilities have gained for him the respect of all. Kind to every one, he goes about doing good, silent and unseen. Again I touch upon the circle of honoured names I must not mention; but I would fain acknowledge his generosity and affectionate interest which make it possible for me to go to college.

Thus it is that my friends have made the story of my life. In a thousand ways they have turned my limitations into beautiful privileges, and enabled me to walk serene and happy in the shadow cast by my deprivation.

Helen Keller Through the Years

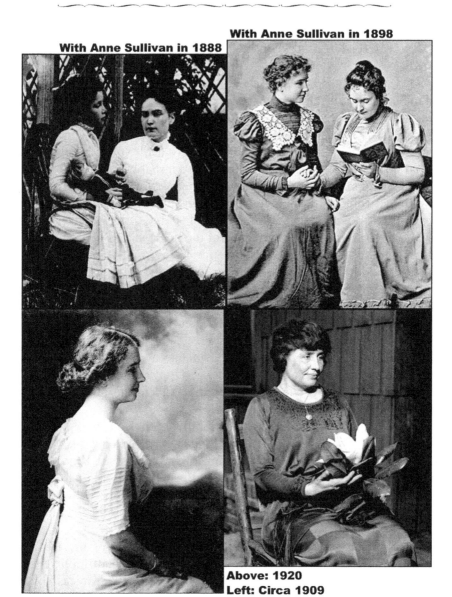

With Anne Sullivan in 1888

With Anne Sullivan in 1898

Above: 1920
Left: Circa 1909

THE WORLD I LIVE IN

Copyright, 1907, by The Whitman Studio
Helen Keller in Her Study

To Henry H. Rogers
My Dear Friend Of Many Years

PREFACE

THE ESSAYS and the poem in this book appeared originally in the "Century Magazine," the essays under the titles "A Chat About the Hand," "Sense and Sensibility," and "My Dreams." Mr. Gilder suggested the articles, and I thank him for his kind interest and encouragement. But he must also accept the responsibility which goes with my gratitude. For it is owing to his wish and that of other editors that I talk so much about myself.

Every book is in a sense autobiographical. But while other self-recording creatures are permitted at least to seem to change the subject, apparently nobody cares what I think of the tariff, the conservation of our natural resources, or the conflicts which revolve about the name of Dreyfus. If I offer to reform the education system of the world, my editorial friends say, "That is interesting. But will you please tell us what idea you had of goodness and beauty when you were six years old?" First they ask me to tell the life of the child who is mother to the woman. Then they make me my own daughter and ask for an account of grown-up sensations. Finally I am requested to write about my dreams, and thus I become an anachronical grandmother; for it is the special privilege of old age to relate dreams. The editors are so kind that they are no doubt right in thinking that nothing I have to say about the affairs of the universe would be interesting. But until they give me opportunity to write about matters that are not-me, the world must go on uninstructed and unreformed, and I can only do my best with the one small subject upon which I am allowed to discourse.

In "The Chant of Darkness" I did not intend to set up as a poet. I thought I was writing prose, except for the magnificent passage from Job which I was paraphrasing. But this part seemed to my friends to separate itself from the exposition, and I made it into a kind of poem.

H. K.

CONTENTS

Chapter I:	The Seeing Hand	80
Chapter II:	The Hands of Others	83
Chapter III:	The Hand of the Race	87
Chapter IV:	The Power of Touch	89
Chapter V:	The Finer Vibrations	93
Chapter VI:	Smell, the Fallen Angel	97
Chapter VII:	Relative Values of the Senses	101
Chapter VIII:	The Five-sensed World	103
Chapter IX:	Inward Visions	105
Chapter X:	Analogies in Sense Perception	108
Chapter XI:	Before the Soul Dawn	111
Chapter XII:	The Larger Sanctions	113
Chapter XIII:	The Dream World	117
Chapter XIV:	Dreams and Reality	123
Chapter XV:	A Waking Dream	125
	A Chant Of Darkness	131

ILLUSTRATIONS

Helen Keller In Her Study	(above) 77
The Medallion	84
"Listening" To The Trees	96
The Little Boy Next Door	106

I
THE SEEING HAND

I HAVE just touched my dog. He was rolling on the grass, with pleasure in every muscle and limb. I wanted to catch a picture of him in my fingers, and I touched him as lightly as I would cobwebs; but lo, his fat body revolved, stiffened and solidified into an upright position, and his tongue gave my hand a lick! He pressed close to me, as if he were fain to crowd himself into my hand. He loved it with his tail, with his paw, with his tongue. If he could speak, I believe he would say with me that paradise is attained by touch; for in touch is all love and intelligence.

This small incident started me on a chat about hands, and if my chat is fortunate I have to thank my dog-star. In any case, it is pleasant to have something to talk about that no one else has monopolized; it is like making a new path in the trackless woods, blazing the trail where no foot has pressed before. I am glad to take you by the hand and lead you along an untrodden way into a world where the hand is supreme. But at the very outset we encounter a difficulty. You are so accustomed to light, I fear you will stumble when I try to guide you through the land of darkness and silence. The blind are not supposed to be the best of guides. Still, though I cannot warrant not to lose you, I promise that you shall not be led into fire or water, or fall into a deep pit. If you will follow me patiently, you will find that "there's a sound so fine, nothing lives 'twixt it and silence," and that there is more meant in things than meets the eye.

My hand is to me what your hearing and sight together are to you. In large measure we travel the same highways, read the same books, speak the same language, yet our experiences are different. All my comings and goings turn on the hand as on a pivot. It is the hand that binds me to the world of men and women. The hand is my feeler with which I reach through isolation and darkness and seize every pleasure, every activity that my fingers encounter. With the dropping of a little word from another's hand into mine, a slight flutter of the fingers, began the intelligence, the joy, the fullness of my life. Like Job, I feel as if a hand had made me, fashioned me together round about and moulded my very soul.

In all my experiences and thoughts I am conscious of a hand. Whatever moves me, whatever thrills me, is as a hand that touches me in the dark, and that touch is my reality. You might as well say that a sight which makes you glad, or a blow which brings the stinging tears to your eyes, is unreal as to say that those impressions are unreal which I have accumulated by means of touch. The delicate tremble of a butterfly's wings in my hand, the soft petals of violets curling in the cool folds of their leaves or lifting sweetly out of the meadow-grass, the clear, firm outline of face and limb, the smooth arch of a horse's neck and the velvety touch of his nose—all these, and a thousand resultant combinations, which take shape in my mind, constitute my world.

Ideas make the world we live in, and impressions furnish ideas. My world is built of touch-sensations, devoid of physical colour and sound; but without colour and sound it breathes and throbs with life. Every object is associated in my mind with tactual qualities which, combined in countless ways, give me a sense of power, of beauty, or of incongruity: for with my hands I can feel the comic as well as the beautiful in the outward appearance of things. Remember that you, dependent on your sight, do not realize how many things are tangible. All palpable things are mobile or rigid, solid or liquid, big or small, warm or cold, and these qualities are variously modified. The coolness of a water-lily rounding into bloom is different from the coolness of an evening wind in summer, and different again from the coolness of the rain that soaks into the hearts of growing things and gives them life and body. The velvet of the rose is not that of a ripe peach or of a baby's dimpled cheek. The hardness of the rock is to the hardness of wood what a man's deep bass is to a woman's voice when it is low. What I call beauty I find in certain combinations of all these qualities, and is largely derived from the flow of curved and straight lines which is over all things.

"What does the straight line mean to you?" I think you will ask.

It *means* several things. It symbolizes duty. It seems to have the quality of inexorableness that duty has. When I have something to do that must not be set aside, I feel as if I were going forward in a straight line, bound to arrive somewhere, or go on forever without swerving to the right or to the left.

That is what it means. To escape this moralizing you should ask, "How does the straight line feel?" It feels, as I suppose it looks, straight—a dull thought drawn out endlessly. Eloquence to the touch resides not in straight lines, but in unstraight lines, or in many curved and straight lines together. They appear and disappear, are now deep, now shallow, now broken off or lengthened or swelling. They rise and sink beneath my fingers, they are full of sudden starts and pauses, and their variety is inexhaustible and wonderful. So you see I am not shut out from the region of the beautiful, though my hand cannot perceive the brilliant colours in the sunset or on the mountain, or reach into the blue depths of the sky.

Physics tells me that I am well off in a world which, I am told, knows neither cold nor sound, but is made in terms of size, shape, and inherent qualities; for at least every object appears to my fingers standing solidly right side up, and is not an inverted image on the retina which, I understand, your brain is at infinite though unconscious labour to set back on its feet. A tangible object passes complete into my brain with the warmth of life upon it, and occupies the same place that it does in space; for, without egotism, the mind is as large as the universe. When I think of hills, I think of the upward strength I tread upon. When water is the object of my thought, I feel the cool shock of the plunge and the quick yielding of the waves that crisp and curl and ripple about my body. The pleasing changes of rough and smooth, pliant and rigid, curved and straight in the bark and branches of a tree give the truth to my hand. The immovable rock, with its juts and warped surface, bends beneath my fingers into all manner of grooves and hollows. The bulge of a watermelon and the puffed-up rotundities of squashes that sprout, bud, and ripen in that strange garden planted somewhere behind my fingertips are the ludicrous in my tactual memory and imagination. My fingers are tickled to delight by the soft ripple of a baby's laugh, and find amusement in the lusty crow of the barnyard autocrat. Once I had a pet rooster that used to perch on my knee and stretch his neck and crow. A bird in my hand was then worth two in the—barnyard.

My fingers cannot, of course, get the impression of a large whole at a glance; but I feel the parts, and my mind puts them together. I move around my house, touching object after object in order, before I can form an idea of the entire house. In other people's houses I can touch only what is shown to me—the chief objects of interest, carvings on the wall, or a curious architectural feature, exhibited like the family album. Therefore a house with which I am not familiar has for me, at first, no general effect or harmony of detail. It is not a complete conception, but a collection of object-impressions which, as they come to me, are disconnected and isolated. But my mind is full of associations, sensations, theories, and with them it constructs the house. The process reminds me of the building of Solomon's temple, where was neither saw, nor hammer, nor any tool heard while the stones were being laid one upon another. The silent worker is imagination which decrees reality out of chaos.

Without imagination what a poor thing my world would be! My garden would be a silent patch of earth strewn with sticks of a variety of shapes and smells. But when the eye of my mind is opened to its beauty, the bare ground brightens beneath my feet, and the hedge-row bursts into leaf, and the rose-tree shakes its fragrance everywhere. I know how budding trees look, and I enter into the amorous joy of the mating birds, and this is the miracle of imagination.

Twofold is the miracle when, through my fingers, my imagination reaches forth and meets the imagination of an artist which he has embodied in a sculptured form. Although, compared with the life-warm, mobile face of a friend, the marble is cold and pulseless and unresponsive, yet it is beautiful to my hand. Its flowing curves and bendings are a real pleasure; only breath is wanting; but under the spell of the imagination the marble thrills and becomes the divine reality of the ideal. Imagination puts a sentiment into every line and curve, and the statue in my touch is indeed the goddess herself who breathes and moves and enchants.

It is true, however, that some sculptures, even recognized masterpieces, do not please my hand. When I touch what there is of the Winged Victory, it reminds me at first of a headless, limbless dream that flies towards me in an unrestful sleep. The garments of the Victory thrust stiffly out behind, and do not resemble garments that I have felt flying, fluttering, folding, spreading in the wind. But imagination fulfils these imperfections, and straightway the Victory becomes a powerful and spirited figure with the sweep of sea-winds in her robes and the splendour of conquest in her wings.

I find in a beautiful statue perfection of bodily form, the qualities of balance and completeness. The Minerva, hung with a web of poetical allusion, gives me a sense of exhilaration that is almost physical; and I like the luxuriant, wavy hair of Bacchus and Apollo, and the wreath of ivy, so suggestive of pagan holidays.

So imagination crowns the experience of my hands. And they learned their cunning from the wise hand of another, which, itself guided by imagination, led me safely in paths that I knew not, made darkness light before me, and made crooked ways straight.

II
THE HANDS OF OTHERS

THE WARMTH and protectiveness of the hand are most homefelt to me who have always looked to it for aid and joy. I understand perfectly how the Psalmist can lift up his voice with strength and gladness, singing, "I put my trust in the Lord at all times, and his hand shall uphold me, and I shall dwell in safety." In the strength of the human hand, too, there is something divine. I am told that the glance of a beloved eye thrills one from a distance; but there is no distance in the touch of a beloved hand. Even the letters I receive are—

> *Kind letters that betray the heart's deep history,*
> *In which we feel the presence of a hand.*

It is interesting to observe the differences in the hands of people. They show all kinds of vitality, energy, stillness, and cordiality. I never realized how living the hand is until I saw those chill plaster images in Mr. Hutton's collection of casts. The hand I know in life has the fullness of blood in its veins, and is elastic with spirit. How different dear Mr. Hutton's hand was from its dull, insensate image! To me the cast lacks the very form of the hand. Of the many casts in Mr. Hutton's collection I did not recognize any, not even my own. But a loving hand I never forget. I remember in my fingers the large hands of Bishop Brooks, brimful of tenderness and a strong man's joy. If you were deaf and blind, and could have held Mr. Jefferson's hand, you would have seen in it a face and heard a kind voice unlike any other you have known. Mark Twain's hand is full of whimsies and the drollest humours, and while you hold it the drollery changes to sympathy and championship.

Copyright, 1907, by the Whitman Studio

The Medallion The bas-relief on the wall is a portrait of the Queen Dowager of Spain, which Her Majesty had made for Miss Keller

I am told that the words I have just written do not "describe" the hands of my friends, but merely endow them with the kindly human qualities which I know they possess, and which language conveys in abstract words. The criticism implies that I am not giving the primary truth of what I feel; but how otherwise do descriptions in books I read, written by men who can see, render the visible look of a face? I read that a face is strong, gentle; that it is full of patience, of intellect; that it is fine, sweet, noble, beautiful. Have I not the same right to use these words in describing what I feel as you have in describing what you see? They express truly what I feel in the hand. I am seldom conscious of physical qualities, and I do not remember whether the fingers of a hand are short or long, or the skin is moist or dry. No more can you, without conscious effort, recall the details of a face, even when you have seen it many times. If you do recall the features, and say that an eye is blue, a chin sharp, a nose short, or a cheek sunken, I fancy that you do not succeed well in giving the impression of the person,—not so well as when you interpret at once to the heart the essential moral qualities of the face—its humour, gravity, sadness, spirituality. If I should tell you in physical terms how a hand feels, you would be no wiser for my account than a blind man to whom you describe a face in detail. Remember that when a blind man recovers his sight, he does not recognize the commonest thing that has been familiar to his touch, the dearest face intimate to his fingers, and it does not help him at all that things and people have been described to him again and again. So you, who are untrained of touch, do not recognize a hand by the grasp; and so, too, any description I might give would fail to make you acquainted with a friendly hand which my fingers have often folded about, and which my affection translates to my memory.

I cannot describe hands under any class or type; there is no democracy of hands. Some hands tell me that they do everything with the maximum of bustle and noise. Other hands are fidgety and unadvised, with nervous, fussy fingers which indicate a nature sensitive to the little pricks of daily life. Sometimes I recognize with foreboding the kindly but stupid hand of one who tells with many words news that is no news. I have met a bishop with a jocose hand, a humourist with a hand of leaden gravity, a man of pretentious valour with a timorous hand, and a quiet, apologetic man with a fist of iron. When I was a little girl I was taken to see[A] a woman who was blind and paralysed. I shall never forget how she held out her small, trembling hand and pressed sympathy into mine. My eyes fill with tears as I think of her. The weariness, pain, darkness, and sweet patience were all to be felt in her thin, wasted, groping, loving hand.

Few people who do not know me will understand, I think, how much I get of the mood of a friend who is engaged in oral conversation with somebody else. My hand follows his motions; I touch his hand, his arm, his face. I can tell when he is full of glee over a good joke which has not been repeated to me, or when he is telling a lively story. One of my friends is rather aggressive, and his hand always announces the coming of a dispute. By his impatient jerk I know he has argument ready for some one. I have felt him start as a sudden recollection or a new idea shot through his mind. I have felt grief in his hand. I have felt his soul wrap itself in darkness majestically as in a garment. Another friend has positive, emphatic hands which show great pertinacity of opinion. She is the only person I know who emphasizes her spelled words and accents them as she emphasizes and accents her spoken words when I read her

---

[A] The excellent proof-reader has put a query to my use of the word "see." If I had said "visit," he would have asked no questions, yet what does "visit" mean but "see" (*visitare*)? Later I will try to defend myself for using as much of the English language as

lips. I like this varied emphasis better than the monotonous pound of unmodulated people who hammer their meaning into my palm.

Some hands, when they clasp yours, beam and bubble over with gladness. They throb and expand with life. Strangers have clasped my hand like that of a long-lost sister. Other people shake hands with me as if with the fear that I may do them mischief. Such persons hold out civil finger-tips which they permit you to touch, and in the moment of contract they retreat, and inwardly you hope that you will not be called upon again to take that hand of "dormouse valour." It betokens a prudish mind, ungracious pride, and not seldom mistrust. It is the antipode to the hand of those who have large, lovable natures.

The handshake of some people makes you think of accident and sudden death. Contrast this ill-boding hand with the quick, skilful, quiet hand of a nurse whom I remember with affection because she took the best care of my teacher. I have clasped the hands of some rich people that spin not and toil not, and yet are not beautiful. Beneath their soft, smooth roundness what a chaos of undeveloped character!

I am sure there is no hand comparable to the physician's in patient skill, merciful gentleness and splendid certainty. No wonder that Ruskin finds in the sure strokes of the surgeon the perfection of control and delicate precision for the artist to emulate. If the physician is a man of great nature, there will be healing for the spirit in his touch. This magic touch of well-being was in the hand of a dear friend of mine who was our doctor in sickness and health. His happy cordial spirit did his patients good whether they needed medicine or not.

As there are many beauties of the face, so the beauties of the hand are many. Touch has its ecstasies. The hands of people of strong individuality and sensitiveness are wonderfully mobile. In a glance of their finger-tips they express many shades of thought. Now and again I touch a fine, graceful, supple-wristed hand which spells with the same beauty and distinction that you must see in the handwriting of some highly cultivated people. I wish you could see how prettily little children spell in my hand. They are wild flowers of humanity, and their finger motions wild flowers of speech.

All this is my private science of palmistry, and when I tell your fortune it is by no mysterious intuition or gipsy witchcraft, but by natural, explicable recognition of the embossed character in your hand. Not only is the hand as easy to recognize as the face, but it reveals its secrets more openly and unconsciously. People control their countenances, but the hand is under no such restraint. It relaxes and becomes listless when the spirit is low and dejected; the muscles tighten when the mind is excited or the heart glad; and permanent qualities stand written on it all the time.

III
THE HAND OF THE RACE

LOOK IN your "Century Dictionary," or if you are blind, ask your teacher to do it for you, and learn how many idioms are made on the idea of hand, and how many words are formed from the Latin root *manus*—enough words to name all the essential affairs of life. "Hand," with quotations and compounds, occupies twenty-four columns, eight pages of this dictionary. The hand is defined as "the organ of apprehension." How perfectly the definition fits my case in both senses of the word "apprehend"! With my hand I seize and hold all that I find in the three worlds—physical, intellectual, and spiritual.

Think how man has regarded the world in terms of the hand. All life is divided between what lies *on one hand* and on the other. The products of skill are *manu*factures. The conduct of affairs is *man*agement. History seems to be the record—alas for our chronicles of war!—of the *man*œuvres of armies. But the history of peace, too, the narrative of labour in the field, the forest, and the vineyard, is written in the victorious sign *manual*—the sign of the hand that has conquered the wilderness. The labourer himself is called a *hand*. In *man*acle and *manu*mission we read the story of human slavery and freedom.

The minor idioms are myriad; but I will not recall too many, lest you cry, "Hands off!" I cannot desist, however, from this word-game until I have set down a few. Whatever is not one's own by first possession is *second-hand*. That is what I am told my knowledge is. But my well-meaning friends come to my defence, and, not content with endowing me with natural *first-hand* knowledge which is rightfully mine, ascribe to me a preternatural sixth sense and credit to miracles and heaven-sent compensations all that I have won and discovered with my good right hand. And with my left hand too; for with that I read, and it is as true and honourable as the other. By what half-development of human power has the left hand been neglected? When we arrive at the acme of civilization shall we not all be ambidextrous, and in our *hand-to-hand* contests against difficulties shall we not be doubly triumphant? It occurs to me, by the way, that when my teacher was training my unreclaimed spirit, her struggle against the powers of darkness, with the stout arm of discipline and the light of the manual alphabet, was in two senses a hand-to-hand conflict.

No essay would be complete without quotations from Shakspere. In the field which, in the presumption of my youth, I thought was my own he has reaped before me. In almost every play there are passages where the hand plays a part. Lady Macbeth's heart-broken soliloquy over her little hand, from which all the perfumes of Arabia will not wash the stain, is the most pitiful moment in the tragedy. Mark Antony rewards Scarus, the bravest of his soldiers, by asking Cleopatra to give him her hand: "Commend unto his lips thy favouring hand." In a different mood he is enraged because Thyreus, whom he despises, has presumed to kiss the hand of the queen, "my playfellow, the kingly seal of high hearts." When Cleopatra is threatened with the humiliation of gracing Cæsar's triumph, she snatches a dagger, exclaiming, "I will trust my resolution and my good hands." With the same swift instinct, Cassius trusts to his hands when he stabs Cæsar: "Speak, hands, for me!" "Let me kiss your hand," says the blind Gloster to Lear. "Let me wipe it first," replies the broken old king; "it smells of mortality." How charged is this single touch with sad meaning! How it opens our eyes to the fearful purging Lear has undergone, to learn that royalty is no defence against ingratitude and cruelty! Gloster's exclamation about his son, "Did I but live to see thee in my touch, I'd say I had eyes again," is as true to a pulse within me as the grief he feels. The ghost in "Hamlet" recites the wrongs from which springs the tragedy:

> *Thus was I, sleeping, by a brother's hand.*
> *At once of life, of crown, of queen dispatch'd.*

How that passage in "Othello" stops your breath—that passage full of bitter double intention in which Othello's suspicion tips with evil what he says about Desdemona's hand; and she in innocence answers only the innocent meaning of his words: "For 'twas that hand that gave away my heart."

Not all Shakspere's great passages about the hand are tragic. Remember the light play of words in "Romeo and Juliet" where the dialogue, flying nimbly back and forth, weaves a pretty sonnet about the hand. And who knows the hand, if not the lover?

The touch of the hand is in every chapter of the Bible. Why, you could almost rewrite Exodus as the story of the hand. Everything is done by the hand of the Lord and of Moses. The oppression of the Hebrews is translated thus: "The hand of Pharaoh was heavy upon the Hebrews." Their departure out of the land is told in these vivid words: "The Lord brought the children of Israel out of the house of bondage with a strong hand and a stretched-out arm." At the stretching out of the hand of Moses the waters of the Red Sea part and stand all on a heap. When the Lord lifts his hand in anger, thousands perish in the wilderness. Every act, every decree in the history of Israel, as indeed in the history of the human race, is sanctioned by the hand. Is it not used in the great moments of swearing, blessing, cursing, smiting, agreeing, marrying, building, destroying? Its sacredness is in the law that no sacrifice is valid unless the sacrificer lay his hand upon the head of the victim. The congregation lay their hands on the heads of those who are sentenced to death. How terrible the dumb condemnation of their hands must be to the condemned! When Moses builds the altar on Mount Sinai, he is commanded to use no tool, but rear it with his own hands. Earth, sea, sky, man, and all lower animals are holy unto the Lord because he has formed them with his hand. When the Psalmist considers the heavens and the earth, he exclaims: "What is man, O Lord, that thou art mindful of him? For thou hast made him to have dominion over the works of thy hands." The supplicating gesture of the hand always accompanies the spoken prayer, and with clean hands goes the pure heart.

Christ comforted and blessed and healed and wrought many miracles with his hands. He touched the eyes of the blind, and they were opened. When Jairus sought him, overwhelmed with grief, Jesus went and laid his hands on the ruler's daughter, and she awoke from the sleep of death to her father's love. You also remember how he healed the crooked woman. He said to her, "Woman, thou art loosed from thine infirmity," and he laid his hands on her, and immediately she was made straight, and she glorified God.

Look where we will, we find the hand in time and history, working, building, inventing, bringing civilization out of barbarism. The hand symbolizes power and the excellence of work. The mechanic's hand, that minister of elemental forces, the hand that hews, saws, cuts, builds, is useful in the world equally with the delicate hand that paints a wild flower or moulds a Grecian urn, or the hand of a statesman that writes a law. The eye cannot say to the hand, "I have no need of thee." Blessed be the hand! Thrice blessed be the hands that work!

IV
THE POWER OF TOUCH

SOME MONTHS ago, in a newspaper which announced the publication of the "Matilda Ziegler Magazine for the Blind," appeared the following paragraph:

"Many poems and stories must be omitted because they deal with sight. Allusion to moonbeams, rainbows, starlight, clouds, and beautiful scenery may not be printed, because they serve to emphasize the blind man's sense of his affliction."

That is to say, I may not talk about beautiful mansions and gardens because I am poor. I may not read about Paris and the West Indies because I cannot visit them in their territorial reality. I may not dream of heaven because it is possible that I may never go there. Yet a venturesome spirit impels me to use words of sight and sound whose meaning I can guess only from analogy and fancy. This hazardous game is half the delight, the frolic, of daily life. I glow as I read of splendours which the eye alone can survey. Allusions to moonbeams and clouds do not emphasize the sense of my affliction: they carry my soul beyond affliction's narrow actuality.

Critics delight to tell us what we cannot do. They assume that blindness and deafness sever us completely from the things which the seeing and the hearing enjoy, and hence they assert we have no moral right to talk about beauty, the skies, mountains, the song of birds, and colours. They declare that the very sensations we have from the sense of touch are "vicarious," as though our friends felt the sun for us! They deny *a priori* what they have not seen and I have felt. Some brave doubters have gone so far even as to deny my existence. In order, therefore, that I may know that I exist, I resort to Descartes's method: "I think, therefore I am." Thus I am metaphysically established, and I throw upon the doubters the burden of proving my non-existence. When we consider how little has been found out about the mind, is it not amazing that any one should presume to define what one can know or cannot know? I admit that there are innumerable marvels in the visible universe unguessed by me. Likewise, O confident critic, there are a myriad sensations perceived by me of which you do not dream.

Necessity gives to the eye a precious power of seeing, and in the same way it gives a precious power of feeling to the whole body. Sometimes it seems as if the very substance of my flesh were so many eyes looking out at will upon a world new created every day. The silence and darkness which are said to shut me in, open my door most hospitably to countless sensations that distract, inform, admonish, and amuse. With my three trusty guides, touch, smell, and taste, I make many excursions into the borderland of experience which is in sight of the city of Light. Nature accommodates itself to every man's necessity. If the eye is maimed, so that it does not see the beauteous face of day, the touch becomes more poignant and discriminating. Nature proceeds through practice to strengthen and augment the remaining senses. For this reason the blind often hear with greater ease and distinctness than other people. The sense of smell becomes almost a new faculty to penetrate the tangle and vagueness of things. Thus, according to an immutable law, the senses assist and reinforce one another.

It is not for me to say whether we see best with the hand or the eye. I only know that the world I see with my fingers is alive, ruddy, and satisfying. Touch brings the blind many sweet certainties which our more fortunate fellows miss, because their sense of touch is uncultivated. When they look at things, they put their hands in their pockets. No doubt that is one reason why their knowledge is often so vague, inaccurate, and useless. It is probable, too, that our knowledge of phenomena beyond the reach of the hand is equally imperfect. But, at all events, we behold them through a golden mist of fantasy.

There is nothing, however, misty or uncertain about what we can touch. Through the sense of touch I know the faces of friends, the illimitable variety of straight and curved lines, all surfaces, the exuberance of the soil, the delicate shapes of flowers, the noble forms of trees, and the range of mighty winds. Besides objects, surfaces, and atmospherical changes, I perceive countless vibrations. I derive much knowledge of everyday matter from the jars and jolts which are to be felt everywhere in the house.

Footsteps, I discover, vary tactually according to the age, the sex, and the manners of the walker. It is impossible to mistake a child's patter for the tread of a grown person. The step of the young man, strong and free, differs from the heavy, sedate tread of the middle-aged, and from the step of the old man, whose feet drag along the floor, or beat it with slow, faltering accents. On a bare floor a girl walks with a rapid, elastic rhythm which is quite distinct from the graver step of the elderly woman. I have laughed over the creak of new shoes and the clatter of a stout maid performing a jig in the kitchen. One day, in the dining-room of an hotel, a tactual dissonance arrested my attention. I sat still and listened with my feet. I found that two waiters were walking back and forth, but not with the same gait. A band was playing, and I could feel the music-waves along the floor. One of the waiters walked in time to the band, graceful and light, while the other disregarded the music and rushed from table to table to the beat of some discord in his own mind. Their steps reminded me of a spirited war-steed harnessed with a cart-horse.

Often footsteps reveal in some measure the character and the mood of the walker. I feel in them firmness and indecision, hurry and deliberation, activity and laziness, fatigue, carelessness, timidity, anger, and sorrow. I am most conscious of these moods and traits in persons with whom I am familiar.

Footsteps are frequently interrupted by certain jars and jerks, so that I know when one kneels, kicks, shakes something, sits down, or gets up. Thus I follow to some extent the actions of people about me and the changes of their postures. Just now a thick, soft patter of bare, padded feet and a slight jolt told me that my dog had jumped on the chair to look out of the window. I do not, however, allow him to go uninvestigated; for occasionally I feel the same motion, and find him, not on the chair, but trespassing on the sofa.

When a carpenter works in the house or in the barn near by, I know by the slanting, up-and-down, toothed vibration, and the ringing concussion of blow upon blow, that he is sawing or hammering. If I am near enough, a certain vibration, travelling back and forth along a wooden surface, brings me the information that he is using a plane.

A slight flutter on the rug tells me that a breeze has blown my papers off the table. A round thump is a signal that a pencil has rolled on the floor. If a book falls, it gives a flat thud. A wooden rap on the balustrade announces that dinner is ready. Many of these vibrations are obliterated out of doors. On a lawn or the road, I can feel only running, stamping, and the rumble of wheels.

By placing my hand on a person's lips and throat, I gain an idea of many specific vibrations, and interpret them: a boy's chuckle, a man's "Whew!" of surprise, the "Hem!" of annoyance or perplexity, the moan of pain, a scream, a whisper, a rasp, a sob, a choke, and a gasp. The utterances of animals, though wordless, are eloquent to me—the cat's purr, its mew, its angry, jerky, scolding spit; the dog's bow-wow of warning or of joyous welcome, its yelp of despair, and its contented snore; the cow's moo; a monkey's chatter; the snort of a horse; the lion's roar, and the terrible snarl of the tiger. Perhaps I ought to add, for the benefit of the critics and doubters who may peruse this essay, that with my own hands I have felt all these sounds. From my childhood to the present day I have availed myself of every opportunity to visit zoological gardens, menageries, and the circus, and all the animals, except the tiger, have talked into my hand. I have touched the tiger only in a museum, where he is as harmless as a lamb. I have, however, heard him talk by putting my hand on the bars of his cage. I have touched several lions in the flesh, and felt them roar royally, like a cataract over rocks.

To continue, I know the *plop* of liquid in a pitcher. So if I spill my milk, I have not the excuse of ignorance. I am also familiar with the pop of a cork, the sputter of a flame, the tick-tack of the clock, the metallic swing of the windmill, the laboured rise and fall of the pump, the voluminous spurt of the hose, the deceptive tap of the breeze at door and window, and many other vibrations past computing.

There are tactual vibrations which do not belong to skin-touch. They penetrate the skin, the nerves, the bones, like pain, heat, and cold. The beat of a drum smites me through from the chest to the shoulder-blades. The din of the train, the bridge, and grinding machinery retains its "old-man-of-the-sea" grip upon me long after its cause has been left behind. If vibration and motion combine in my touch for any length of time, the earth seems to run away while I stand still. When I step off the train, the platform whirls round, and I find it difficult to walk steadily.

Every atom of my body is a vibroscope. But my sensations are not infallible. I reach out, and my fingers meet something furry, which jumps about, gathers itself together as if to spring, and acts like an animal. I pause a moment for caution. I touch it again more firmly, and find it is a fur coat fluttering and flapping in the wind. To me, as to you, the earth seems motionless, and the sun appears to move; for the rays of the afternoon withdraw more and more, as they touch my face, until the air becomes cool. From this I understand how it is that the shore seems to recede as you sail away from it. Hence I feel no incredulity when you say that parallel lines appear to converge, and the earth and sky to meet. My few senses long ago revealed to me their imperfections and deceptivity.

Not only are the senses deceptive, but numerous usages in our language indicate that people who have five senses find it difficult to keep their functions distinct. I understand that we hear views, see tones, taste music. I am told that voices have colour. Tact, which I have supposed to be a matter of nice perception, turns out to be a matter of taste. Judging from the large use of the word, taste appears to be the most important of all the senses. Taste governs the great and small conventions of life. Certainly the language of the senses is full of contradictions, and my fellows who have five doors to their house are not more surely at home in themselves than I. May I not, then, be excused if this account of my sensations lacks precision?

V
THE FINER VIBRATIONS

I HAVE spoken of the numerous jars and jolts which daily minister to my faculties. The loftier and grander vibrations which appeal to my emotions are varied and abundant. I listen with awe to the roll of the thunder and the muffled avalanche of sound when the sea flings itself upon the shore. And I love the instrument by which all the diapasons of the ocean are caught and released in surging floods—the many-voiced organ. If music could be seen, I could point where the organ-notes go, as they rise and fall, climb up and up, rock and sway, now loud and deep, now high and stormy, anon soft and solemn, with lighter vibrations interspersed between and running across them. I should say that organ-music fills to an ecstasy the act of feeling.

There is tangible delight in other instruments, too. The violin seems beautifully alive as it responds to the lightest wish of the master. The distinction between its notes is more delicate than between the notes of the piano.

I enjoy the music of the piano most when I touch the instrument. If I keep my hand on the piano-case, I detect tiny quavers, returns of melody, and the hush that follows. This explains to me how sound can die away to the listening ear:

> ... *How thin and clear,*
> *And thinner, clearer, farther going!*
> *O sweet and far from cliff and scar*
> *The horns of Elfland faintly blowing!*

I am able to follow the dominant spirit and mood of the music. I catch the joyous dance as it bounds over the keys, the slow dirge, the reverie. I thrill to the fiery sweep of notes crossed by thunderous tones in the "Walküre," where *Wotan* kindles the dread flames that guard the sleeping *Brunhild*. How wonderful is the instrument on which a great musician sings with his hands! I have never succeeded in distinguishing one composition from another. I think this is impossible; but the concentration and strain upon my attention would be so great that I doubt if the pleasure derived would be commensurate to the effort.

Nor can I distinguish easily a tune that is sung. But by placing my hand on another's throat and cheek, I enjoy the changes of the voice. I know when it is low or high, clear or muffled, sad or cheery. The thin, quavering sensation of an old voice differs in my touch from the sensation of a young voice. A Southerner's drawl is quite unlike the Yankee twang. Sometimes the flow and ebb of a voice is so enchanting that my fingers quiver with exquisite pleasure, even if I do not understand a word that is spoken.

On the other hand, I am exceedingly sensitive to the harshness of noises like grinding, scraping, and the hoarse creak of rusty locks. Fog-whistles are my vibratory nightmares. I have stood near a bridge in process of construction, and felt the tactual din, the rattle of heavy masses of stone, the roll of loosened earth, the rumble of engines, the dumping of dirt-cars, the triple blows of vulcan hammers. I can also smell the fire-pots, the tar and cement. So I have a vivid idea of mighty labours in steel and stone, and I believe that I am acquainted with all the fiendish noises which can be made by man or machinery. The whack of heavy falling bodies, the sudden shivering splinter of chopped logs, the crystal shatter of pounded ice, the crash of a tree hurled to the earth by a hurricane, the irrational, persistent chaos of noise made by switching freight-trains, the explosion of gas, the blasting of stone, and the terrific grinding of rock upon rock which precedes the collapse—all these have been in my touch-experience, and contribute to my idea of Bedlam, of a battle, a waterspout, an earthquake, and other enormous accumulations of sound.

Touch brings me into contact with the traffic and manifold activity of the city. Besides the bustle and crowding of people and the nondescript grating and electric howling of street-cars, I am conscious of exhalations from many different kinds of shops; from automobiles, drays, horses, fruit stands, and many varieties of smoke.

> *Odours strange and musty,*
> *The air sharp and dusty*
> *With lime and with sand,*
> *That no one can stand,*
> *Make the street impassable,*
> *The people irascible,*
> *Until every one cries,*
> *As he trembling goes*
> *With the sight of his eyes*
> *And the scent of his nose*
> *Quite stopped—or at least much diminished—*
> *"Gracious! when will this city be finished?"* [B]

The city is interesting; but the tactual silence of the country is always most welcome after the din of town and the irritating concussions of the train. How noiseless and undisturbing are the demolition, the repairs and the alterations, of nature! With no sound of hammer or saw or stone severed from stone, but a music of rustles and ripe thumps on the grass come the fluttering leaves and mellow fruits which the wind tumbles all day from the branches. Silently all droops, all withers, all is poured back into the earth that it may recreate; all sleeps while the busy architects of day and night ply their silent work elsewhere. The same serenity reigns when all at once the soil yields up a newly wrought creation. Softly the ocean of grass, moss, and flowers rolls surge upon surge across the earth.

[B] George Arnold

Curtains of foliage drape the bare branches. Great trees make ready in their sturdy hearts to receive again birds which occupy their spacious chambers to the south and west. Nay, there is no place so lowly that it may not lodge some happy creature. The meadow brook undoes its icy fetters with rippling notes, gurgles, and runs free. And all this is wrought in less than two months to the music of nature's orchestra, in the midst of balmy incense.

"Listening" to the Trees

The thousand soft voices of the earth have truly found their way to me—the small rustle in tufts of grass, the silky swish of leaves, the buzz of insects, the hum of bees in blossoms I have plucked, the flutter of a bird's wings after his bath, and the slender rippling vibration of water running over pebbles. Once having been felt, these loved voices rustle, buzz, hum, flutter, and ripple in my thought forever, an undying part of happy memories.

Between my experiences and the experiences of others there is no gulf of mute space which I may not bridge. For I have endlessly varied, instructive contacts with all the world, with life, with the atmosphere whose radiant activity enfolds us all. The thrilling energy of the all-encasing air is warm and rapturous. Heat-waves and sound-waves play upon my face in infinite variety and combination, until I am able to surmise what must be the myriad sounds that my senseless ears have not heard.

The air varies in different regions, at different seasons of the year, and even different hours of the day. The odorous, fresh sea-breezes are distinct from the fitful breezes along river banks, which are humid and freighted with inland smells. The bracing, light, dry air of the mountains can never be mistaken for the pungent salt air of the ocean. The air of winter is dense, hard, compressed. In the spring it has new vitality. It is light, mobile, and laden with a thousand palpitating odours from earth, grass, and sprouting leaves. The air of midsummer is dense, saturated, or dry and burning, as if it came from a furnace. When a cool breeze brushes the sultry stillness, it brings fewer odours than in May, and frequently the odour of a coming tempest. The avalanche of coolness which sweeps through the low-hanging air bears little resemblance to the stinging coolness of winter.

The rain of winter is raw, without odour, and dismal. The rain of spring is brisk, fragrant, charged with life-giving warmth. I welcome it delightedly as it visits the earth, enriches the streams, waters the hills abundantly, makes the furrows soft with showers for the seed, elicits a perfume which I cannot breathe deep enough. Spring rain is beautiful, impartial, lovable. With pearly drops it washes every leaf on tree and bush, ministers equally to salutary herbs and noxious growths, searches out every living thing that needs its beneficence.

The senses assist and reinforce each other to such an extent that I am not sure whether touch or smell tells me the most about the world. Everywhere the river of touch is joined by the brooks of odour-perception. Each season has its distinctive odours. The spring is earthy and full of sap. July is rich with the odour of ripening grain and hay. As the season advances, a crisp, dry, mature odour predominates, and golden-rod, tansy, and everlastings mark the onward march of the year. In autumn, soft, alluring scents fill the air, floating from thicket, grass, flower, and tree, and they tell me of time and change, of death and life's renewal, desire and its fulfilment.

VI
SMELL, THE FALLEN ANGEL

FOR SOME inexplicable reason the sense of smell does not hold the high position it deserves among its sisters. There is something of the fallen angel about it. When it woos us with woodland scents and beguiles us with the fragrance of lovely gardens, it is admitted frankly to our discourse. But when it gives us warning of something noxious in our vicinity, it is treated as if the demon had got the upper hand of the angel, and is relegated to outer darkness, punished for its faithful service. It is most difficult to keep the true significance of words when one discusses the prejudices of mankind, and I find it hard to give an account of odour-perceptions which shall be at once dignified and truthful.

In my experience smell is most important, and I find that there is high authority for the nobility of the sense which we have neglected and disparaged. It is recorded that the Lord commanded that incense be burnt before him continually with a sweet savour. I doubt if there is any sensation arising from sight more delightful than the odours which filter through sun-warmed, wind-tossed branches, or the tide of scents which swells, subsides, rises again wave on wave, filling the wide world with invisible sweetness. A whiff of the universe makes us dream of worlds we have never seen, recalls in a flash entire epochs of our dearest experience. I never smell daisies without living over again the ecstatic mornings that my teacher and I spent wandering in the fields, while I learned new words and the names of things. Smell is a potent wizard that transports us across a thousand miles and all the years we have lived. The odour of fruits wafts me to my Southern home, to my childish frolics in the peach orchard. Other odours, instantaneous and fleeting, cause my heart to dilate joyously or contract with remembered grief. Even as I think of smells, my nose is full of scents that start awake sweet memories of summers gone and ripening grain fields far away.

The faintest whiff from a meadow where the new-mown hay lies in the hot sun displaces the here and the now. I am back again in the old red barn. My little friends and I are playing in the haymow. A huge mow it is, packed with crisp, sweet hay, from the top of which the smallest child can reach the straining rafters. In their stalls beneath are the farm animals. Here is Jerry, unresponsive, unbeautiful Jerry, crunching his oats like a true pessimist, resolved to find his feed not good—at least not so good as it ought to be. Again I touch Brownie, eager, grateful little Brownie, ready to leave the juiciest fodder for a pat, straining his beautiful, slender neck for a caress. Near by stands Lady Belle, with sweet, moist mouth, lazily extracting the sealed-up cordial from timothy and clover, and dreaming of deep June pastures and murmurous streams.

The sense of smell has told me of a coming storm hours before there was any sign of it visible. I notice first a throb of expectancy, a slight quiver, a concentration in my nostrils. As the storm draws nearer, my nostrils dilate the better to receive the flood of earth-odours which seem to multiply and extend, until I feel the splash of rain against my cheek. As the tempest departs, receding farther and farther, the odours fade, become fainter and fainter, and die away beyond the bar of space.

I know by smell the kind of house we enter. I have recognized an old-fashioned country house because it has several layers of odours, left by a succession of families, of plants, perfumes, and draperies.

In the evening quiet there are fewer vibrations than in the daytime, and then I rely more largely upon smell. The sulphuric scent of a match tells me that the lamps are being lighted. Later I note the wavering trail of odour that flits about and disappears. It is the curfew signal; the lights are out for the night.

Out of doors I am aware by smell and touch of the ground we tread and the places we pass. Sometimes, when there is no wind, the odours are so grouped that I know the character of the country, and can place a hayfield, a country store, a garden, a barn, a grove of pines, a farmhouse with the windows open.

The other day I went to walk toward a familiar wood. Suddenly a disturbing odour made me pause in dismay. Then followed a peculiar, measured jar, followed by dull, heavy thunder. I understood the odour and the jar only too well. The trees were being cut down. We climbed the stone wall to the left. It borders the wood which I have loved so long that it seems to be my peculiar possession. But to-day an unfamiliar rush of air and an unwonted outburst of sun told me that my tree friends were gone. The place was empty, like a deserted dwelling. I stretched out my hand. Where once stood the steadfast pines, great, beautiful, sweet, my hand touched raw, moist stumps. All about lay broken branches, like the antlers of stricken deer. The fragrant, piled-up sawdust swirled and tumbled about me. An unreasoning resentment flashed through me at this ruthless destruction of the beauty that I love. But there is no anger, no resentment in nature. The air is equally charged with the odours of life and of destruction, for death equally with growth forever ministers to all-conquering life. The sun shines as ever, and the winds riot through the newly opened spaces. I know that a new forest will spring where the old one stood, as beautiful, as beneficent.

Touch sensations are permanent and definite. Odours deviate and are fugitive, changing in their shades, degrees, and location. There is something else in odour which gives me a sense of distance. I should call it horizon—the line where odour and fancy meet at the farthest limit of scent.

Smell gives me more idea than touch or taste of the manner in which sight and hearing probably discharge their functions. Touch seems to reside in the object touched, because there is a contact of surfaces. In smell there is no notion of relievo, and odour seems to reside not in the object smelt, but in the organ. Since I smell a tree at a distance, it is comprehensible to me that a person sees it without touching it. I am not puzzled over the fact that he receives it as an image on his retina without relievo, since my smell perceives the tree as a thin sphere with no fullness or content. By themselves, odours suggest nothing. I must learn by association to judge from them of distance, of place, and of the actions or the surroundings which are the usual occasions for them, just as I am told people judge from colour, light, and sound.

From exhalations I learn much about people. I often know the work they are engaged in. The odours of wood, iron, paint, and drugs cling to the garments of those that work in them. Thus I can distinguish the carpenter from the ironworker, the artist from the mason or the chemist. When a person passes quickly from one place to another I get a scent impression of where he has been—the kitchen, the garden, or the sick-room. I gain pleasurable ideas of freshness and good taste from the odours of soap, toilet water, clean garments, woollen and silk stuffs, and gloves.

I have not, indeed, the all-knowing scent of the hound or the wild animal. None but the halt and the blind need fear my skill in pursuit; for there are other things besides water, stale trails, confusing cross tracks to put me at fault. Nevertheless, human odours are as varied and capable of recognition as hands and faces. The dear odours of those I love are so definite, so unmistakable, that nothing can quite obliterate them. If many years should elapse before I saw an intimate friend again, I think I should recognize his odour instantly in the heart of Africa, as promptly as would my brother that barks.

Once, long ago, in a crowded railway station, a lady kissed me as she hurried by. I had not touched even her dress. But she left a scent with her kiss which gave me a glimpse of her. The years are many since she kissed me. Yet her odour is fresh in my memory.

It is difficult to put into words the thing itself, the elusive person-odour. There seems to be no adequate vocabulary of smells, and I must fall back on approximate phrase and metaphor.

Some people have a vague, unsubstantial odour that floats about, mocking every effort to identify it. It is the will-o'-the-wisp of my olfactive experience. Sometimes I meet one who lacks a distinctive person-scent, and I seldom find such a one lively or entertaining. On the other hand, one who has a pungent odour often possesses great vitality, energy, and vigour of mind.

Masculine exhalations are as a rule stronger, more vivid, more widely differentiated than those of women. In the odour of young men there is something elemental, as of fire, storm, and salt sea. It pulsates with buoyancy and desire. It suggests all things strong and beautiful and joyous, and gives me a sense of physical happiness. I wonder if others observe that all infants have the same scent—pure, simple, undecipherable as their dormant personality. It is not until the age of six or seven that they begin to have perceptible individual odours. These develop and mature along with their mental and bodily powers.

What I have written about smell, especially person-smell, will perhaps be regarded as the abnormal sentiment of one who can have no idea of the "world of reality and beauty which the eye perceives." There are people who are colour-blind, people who are tone-deaf. Most people are smell-blind-and-deaf. We should not condemn a musical composition on the testimony of an ear which cannot distinguish one chord from another, or judge a picture by the verdict of a colour-blind critic. The sensations of smell which cheer, inform, and broaden my life are not less pleasant merely because some critic who treads the wide, bright pathway of the eye has not cultivated his olfactive sense. Without the shy, fugitive, often unobserved sensations and the certainties which taste, smell, and touch give me, I should be obliged to take my conception of the universe wholly from others. I should lack the alchemy by which I now infuse into my world light, colour, and the Protean spark. The sensuous reality which interthreads and supports all the gropings of my imagination would be shattered. The solid earth would melt from under my feet and disperse itself in space. The objects dear to my hands would become formless, dead things, and I should walk among them as among invisible ghosts.

VII
Relative Values of the Senses

I WAS once without the sense of smell and taste for several days. It seemed incredible, this utter detachment from odours, to breathe the air in and observe never a single scent. The feeling was probably similar, though less in degree, to that of one who first loses sight and cannot but expect to see the light again any day, any minute. I knew I should smell again some time. Still, after the wonder had passed off, a loneliness crept over me as vast as the air whose myriad odours I missed. The multitudinous subtle delights that smell makes mine became for a time wistful memories. When I recovered the lost sense, my heart bounded with gladness. It is a fine dramatic touch that Hans Andersen gives to the story of Kay and Gerda in the passage about flowers. Kay, whom the wicked magician's glass has blinded to human love, rushes away fiercely from home when he discovers that the roses have lost their sweetness.

The loss of smell for a few days gave me a clearer idea than I had ever had what it is to be blinded suddenly, helplessly. With a little stretch of the imagination I knew then what it must be when the great curtain shuts out suddenly the light of day, the stars, and the firmament itself. I see the blind man's eyes strain for the light, as he fearfully tries to walk his old rounds, until the unchanging blank that everywhere spreads before him stamps the reality of the dark upon his consciousness.

My temporary loss of smell proved to me, too, that the absence of a sense need not dull the mental faculties and does not distort one's view of the world, and so I reason that blindness and deafness need not pervert the inner order of the intellect. I know that if there were no odours for me I should still possess a considerable part of the world. Novelties and surprises would abound, adventures would thicken in the dark.

In my classification of the senses, smell is a little the ear's inferior, and touch is a great deal the eye's superior. I find that great artists and philosophers agree with me in this. Diderot says:

> Je trouvais que de tous les sens, l'œil était le plus superficiel; l'oreille, le plus orgueilleux; l'odorat, le plus voluptueux; le goût, le plus superstitieux et le plus inconstant; le toucher, le plus profond et le plus philosophe. C

A friend whom I have never seen sends me a quotation from Symonds's "Renaissance in Italy":

> Lorenzo Ghiberti, after describing a piece of antique sculpture he saw in Rome adds, "To express the perfection of learning, mastery, and art displayed in it is beyond the power of language. Its more exquisite beauties could not be discovered by the sight, but only by the touch of the hand passed over it." Of another classic marble at Padua he says, "This statue, when the Christian faith triumphed, was hidden in that place by some gentle soul, who, seeing it so perfect, fashioned with art so wonderful, and with such power of genius, and being moved to reverent pity, caused a sepulchre of bricks to be built, and there within buried the statue, and covered it with a broad slab of stone, that it might not in any way be injured. It has very many sweet beauties which the eyes alone can comprehend not, either by strong or tempered light; only the hand by touching them finds them out."

Hold out your hands to feel the luxury of the sunbeams. Press the soft blossoms against your cheek, and finger their graces of form, their delicate mutability of shape, their pliancy and freshness. Expose your face to the aerial floods that sweep the heavens, "inhale great draughts of space," wonder, wonder at the wind's unwearied activity. Pile note on note the infinite music that flows increasingly to your soul from the tactual sonorities of a thousand branches and tumbling waters. How can the world be shrivelled when this most profound, emotional sense, touch, is faithful to its service? I am sure that if a fairy bade me choose between the sense of light and that of touch, I would not part with the warm, endearing contact of human hands or the wealth of form, the nobility and fullness that press into my palms.

C I found that of the senses, the eye is the most superficial, the ear the most arrogant, smell the most voluptuous, taste the most superstitious and fickle, touch the most profound and the most philosophical.

VIII
THE FIVE-SENSED WORLD

THE POETS have taught us how full of wonders is the night; and the night of blindness has its wonders, too. The only lightless dark is the night of ignorance and insensibility. We differ, blind and seeing, one from another, not in our senses, but in the use we make of them, in the imagination and courage with which we seek wisdom beyond our senses.

It is more difficult to teach ignorance to think than to teach an intelligent blind man to see the grandeur of Niagara. I have walked with people whose eyes are full of light, but who see nothing in wood, sea, or sky, nothing in city streets, nothing in books. What a witless masquerade is this seeing! It were better far to sail forever in the night of blindness, with sense and feeling and mind, than to be thus content with the mere act of seeing. They have the sunset, the morning skies, the purple of distant hills, yet their souls voyage through this enchanted world with a barren stare.

The calamity of the blind is immense, irreparable. But it does not take away our share of the things that count—service, friendship, humour, imagination, wisdom. It is the secret inner will that controls one's fate. We are capable of willing to be good, of loving and being loved, of thinking to the end that we may be wiser. We possess these spirit-born forces equally with all God's children. Therefore we, too, see the lightnings and hear the thunders of Sinai. We, too, march through the wilderness and the solitary place that shall be glad for us, and as we pass, God maketh the desert to blossom like the rose. We, too, go in unto the Promised Land to possess the treasures of the spirit, the unseen permanence of life and nature.

The blind man of spirit faces the unknown and grapples with it, and what else does the world of seeing men do? He has imagination, sympathy, humanity, and these ineradicable existences compel him to share by a sort of proxy in a sense he has not. When he meets terms of colour, light, physiognomy, he guesses, divines, puzzles out their meaning by analogies drawn from the senses he has. I naturally tend to think, reason, draw inferences as if I had five senses instead of three. This tendency is beyond my control; it is involuntary, habitual, instinctive. I cannot compel my mind to say "I feel" instead of "I see" or "I hear." The word "feel" proves on examination to be no less a convention than "see" and "hear" when I seek for words accurately to describe the outward things that affect my three bodily senses. When a man loses a leg, his brain persists in impelling him to use what he has not and yet feels to be there. Can it be that the brain is so constituted that it will continue the activity which animates the sight and the hearing, after the eye and the ear have been destroyed?

It might seem that the five senses would work intelligently together only when resident in the same body. Yet when two or three are left unaided, they reach out for their complements in another body, and find that they yoke easily with the borrowed team. When my hand aches from overtouching, I find relief in the sight of another. When my mind lags, wearied with the strain of forcing out thoughts about dark, musicless, colourless, detached substance, it recovers its elasticity as soon as I resort to the powers of another mind which commands light, harmony, colour. Now, if the five senses will not remain disassociated, the life of the deaf-blind cannot be severed from the life of the seeing, hearing race.

The deaf-blind person may be plunged and replunged like Schiller's diver into seas of the unknown. But, unlike the doomed hero, he returns triumphant, grasping the priceless truth that his mind is not crippled, not limited to the infirmity of his senses. The world of the eye and the ear becomes to him a subject of fateful interest. He seizes every word of sight and hearing because his sensations compel it. Light and colour, of which he has no tactual evidence, he studies fearlessly, believing that all humanly knowable truth is open to him. He is in a position similar to that of the astronomer who, firm, patient, watches a star night after night for many years and feels rewarded if he discovers a single fact about it. The man deaf-blind to ordinary outward things, and the man deaf-blind to the immeasurable universe, are both limited by time and space; but they have made a compact to wring service from their limitations.

The bulk of the world's knowledge is an imaginary construction. History is but a mode of imagining, of making us see civilizations that no longer appear upon the earth. Some of the most significant discoveries in modern science owe their origin to the imagination of men who had neither accurate knowledge nor exact instruments to demonstrate their beliefs. If astronomy had not kept always in advance of the telescope, no one would ever have thought a telescope worth making. What great invention has not existed in the inventor's mind long before he gave it tangible shape?

A more splendid example of imaginative knowledge is the unity with which philosophers start their study of the world. They can never perceive the world in its entire reality. Yet their imagination, with its magnificent allowance for error, its power of treating uncertainty as negligible, has pointed the way for empirical knowledge.

In their highest creative moments the great poet, the great musician cease to use the crude instruments of sight and hearing. They break away from their sense-moorings, rise on strong, compelling wings of spirit far above our misty hills and darkened valleys into the region of light, music, intellect.

What eye hath seen the glories of the New Jerusalem? What ear hath heard the music of the spheres, the steps of time, the strokes of chance, the blows of death? Men have not heard with their physical sense the tumult of sweet voices above the hills of Judea nor seen the heavenly vision; but millions have listened to that spiritual message through many ages.

Our blindness changes not a whit the course of inner realities. Of us it is as true as it is of the seeing that the most beautiful world is always entered through the imagination. If you wish to be something that you are not,—something fine, noble, good,—you shut your eyes, and for one dreamy moment you are that which you long to be.

IX
INWARD VISIONS

ACCORDING TO all art, all nature, all coherent human thought, we know that order, proportion, form, are essential elements of beauty. Now order, proportion, and form, are palpable to the touch. But beauty and rhythm are deeper than sense. They are like love and faith. They spring out of a spiritual process only slightly dependent upon sensations. Order, proportion, form, cannot generate in the mind the abstract idea of beauty, unless there is already a soul intelligence to breathe life into the elements. Many persons, having perfect eyes, are blind in their perceptions. Many persons, having perfect ears, are emotionally deaf. Yet these are the very ones who dare to set limits to the vision of those who, lacking a sense or two, have will, soul, passion, imagination. Faith is a mockery if it teaches us not that we may construct a world unspeakably more complete and beautiful than the material world. And I, too, may construct my better world, for I am a child of God, an inheritor of a fragment of the Mind that created all worlds.

There is a consonance of all things, a blending of all that we know about the material world and the spiritual. It consists for me of all the impressions, vibrations, heat, cold, taste, smell, and the sensations which these convey to the mind, infinitely combined, interwoven with associated ideas and acquired knowledge. No thoughtful person will believe that what I said about the meaning of footsteps is strictly true of mere jolts and jars. It is an array of the spiritual in certain natural elements, tactual beats, and an acquired knowledge of physical habits and moral traits of highly organized human beings. What would odours signify if they were not associated with the time of the year, the place I live in, and the people I know?

The result of such a blending is sometimes a discordant trying of strings far removed from a melody, very far from a symphony. (For the benefit of those who must be reassured, I will say that I have felt a musician tuning his violin, that I have read about a symphony, and so have a fair intellectual perception of my metaphor.) But with training and experience the faculties gather up the stray notes and combine them into a full, harmonious whole. If the person who accomplishes this task is peculiarly gifted, we call him a poet. The blind and the deaf are not great poets, it is true. Yet now and again you find one deaf and blind who has attained to his royal kingdom of beauty.

I have a little volume of poems by a deaf-blind lady, Madame Bertha Galeron. Her poetry has versatility of thought. Now it is tender and sweet, now full of tragic passion and the sternness of destiny. Victor Hugo called her "La Grande Voyante." She has written several plays, two of which have been acted in Paris. The French Academy has crowned her work.

Copyright, 1907, by The Whitman Studio
The Little Boy Next Door

The infinite wonders of the universe are revealed to us in exact measure as we are capable of receiving them. The keenness of our vision depends not on how much we can see, but on how much we feel. Nor yet does mere knowledge create beauty. Nature sings her most exquisite songs to those who love her. She does not unfold her secrets to those who come only to gratify their desire of analysis, to gather facts, but to those who see in her manifold phenomena suggestions of lofty, delicate sentiments.

Am I to be denied the use of such adjectives as "freshness" and "sparkle," "dark" and "gloomy"? I have walked in the fields at early morning. I have felt a rose-bush laden with dew and fragrance. I have felt the curves and graces of my kitten at play. I have known the sweet, shy ways of little children. I have known the sad opposites of all these, a ghastly touch picture. Remember, I have sometimes travelled over a dusty road as far as my feet could go. At a sudden turn I have stepped upon starved, ignoble weeds, and reaching out my hands, I have touched a fair tree out of which a parasite had taken the life like a vampire. I have touched a pretty bird whose soft wings hung limp, whose little heart beat no more. I have wept over the feebleness and deformity of a child, lame, or born blind, or, worse still, mindless. If I had the genius of Thomson, I, too, could depict a "City of Dreadful Night" from mere touch sensations. From contrasts so irreconcilable can we fail to form an idea of beauty and know surely when we meet with loveliness?

Here is a sonnet eloquent of a blind man's power of vision

THE MOUNTAIN TO THE PINE

Thou tall, majestic monarch of the wood,
   That standest where no wild vines dare to creep,
Men call thee old, and say that thou hast stood
   A century upon my rugged steep;
Yet unto me thy life is but a day,
   When I recall the things that I have seen,—
The forest monarchs that have passed away
   Upon the spot where first I saw thy green;
For I am older than the age of man,
   Or all the living things that crawl or creep,
   Or birds of air, or creatures of the deep;
I was the first dim outline of God's plan:
   Only the waters of the restless sea
   And the infinite stars in heaven are old to me.

I am glad my friend Mr. Stedman knew that poem while he was making his Anthology, for knowing it, so fine a poet and critic could not fail to give it a place in his treasure-house of American poetry. The poet, Mr. Clarence Hawkes, has been blind since childhood; yet he finds in nature hints of combinations for his mental pictures. Out of the knowledge and impressions that come to him he constructs a masterpiece which hangs upon the walls of his thought. And into the poet's house come all the true spirits of the world.

It was a rare poet who thought of the mountain as "the first dim outline of God's plan." That is the real wonder of the poem, and not that a blind man should speak so confidently of sky and sea. Our ideas of the sky are an accumulation of touch-glimpses, literary allusions, and the observations of others, with an emotional blending of all. My face feels only a tiny portion of the atmosphere; but I go through continuous space and feel the air at every point, every instant. I have been told about the distances from our earth to the sun, to the other planets, and to the fixed stars. I multiply a thousand times the utmost height and width that my touch compasses, and thus I gain a deep sense of the sky's immensity.

Move me along constantly over water, water, nothing but water, and you give me the solitude, the vastness of ocean which fills the eye. I have been in a little sail-boat on the sea, when the rising tide swept it toward the shore. May I not understand the poet's figure: "The green of spring overflows the earth like a tide"? I have felt the flame of a candle blow and flutter in the breeze. May I not, then, say: "Myriads of fireflies flit hither and thither in the dew-wet grass like little fluttering tapers"?

Combine the endless space of air, the sun's warmth, the clouds that are described to my understanding spirit, the frequent breaking through the soil of a brook or the expanse of the wind-ruffled lake, the tactual undulation of the hills, which I recall when I am far away from them, the towering trees upon trees as I walk by them, the bearings that I try to keep while others tell me the directions of the various points of the scenery, and you will begin to feel surer of my mental landscape. The utmost bound to which my thought will go with clearness is the horizon of my mind. From this horizon I imagine the one which the eye marks.

Touch cannot bridge distance,—it is fit only for the contact of surfaces,—but thought leaps the chasm. For this reason I am able to use words descriptive of objects distant from my senses. I have felt the rondure of the infant's tender form. I can apply this perception to the landscape and to the far-off hills.

X
ANALOGIES IN SENSE PERCEPTION

I HAVE not touched the outline of a star nor the glory of the moon, but I believe that God has set two lights in mind, the greater to rule by day and the lesser by night, and by them I know that I am able to navigate my life-bark, as certain of reaching the haven as he who steers by the North Star. Perhaps my sun shines not as yours. The colours that glorify my world, the blue of the sky, the green of the fields, may not correspond exactly with those you delight in; but they are none the less colour to me. The sun does not shine for my physical eyes, nor does the lightning flash, nor do the trees turn green in the spring; but they have not therefore ceased to exist, any more than the landscape is annihilated when you turn your back on it.

I understand how scarlet can differ from crimson because I know that the smell of an orange is not the smell of a grape-fruit. I can also conceive that colours have shades, and guess what shades are. In smell and taste there are varieties not broad enough to be fundamental; so I call them shades. There are half a dozen roses near me. They all have the unmistakable rose scent; yet my nose tells me that they are not the same. The American Beauty is distinct from the Jacqueminot and La France. Odours in certain grasses fade as really to my sense as certain colours do to yours in the sun. The freshness of a flower in my hand is analogous to the freshness I taste in an apple newly picked. I make use of analogies like these to enlarge my conceptions of colours. Some analogies which I draw between qualities in surface and vibration, taste and smell, are drawn by others between sight, hearing, and touch. This fact encourages me to persevere, to try and bridge the gap between the eye and the hand.

Certainly I get far enough to sympathize with the delight that my kind feel in beauty they see and harmony they hear. This bond between humanity and me is worth keeping, even if the idea on which I base it prove erroneous.

Sweet, beautiful vibrations exist for my touch, even though they travel through other substances than air to reach me. So I imagine sweet, delightful sounds, and the artistic arrangement of them which is called music, and I remember that they travel through the air to the ear, conveying impressions somewhat like mine. I also know what tones are, since they are perceptible tactually in a voice. Now, heat varies greatly in the sun, in the fire, in hands, and in the fur of animals; indeed, there is such a thing for me as a cold sun. So I think of the varieties of light that touch the eye, cold and warm, vivid and dim, soft and glaring, but always light, and I imagine their passage through the air to an extensive sense, instead of to a narrow one like touch. From the experience I have had with voices I guess how the eye distinguishes shades in the midst of light. While I read the lips of a woman whose voice is soprano, I note a low tone or a glad tone in the midst of a high, flowing voice. When I feel my cheeks hot, I know that I am red. I have talked so much and read so much about colours that through no will of my own I attach meanings to them, just as all people attach certain meanings to abstract terms like hope, idealism, monotheism, intellect, which cannot be represented truly by visible objects, but which are understood from analogies between immaterial concepts and the ideas they awaken of external things. The force of association drives me to say that white is exalted and pure, green is exuberant, red suggests love or shame or strength. Without the colour or its equivalent, life to me would be dark, barren, a vast blackness.

Thus through an inner law of completeness my thoughts are not permitted to remain colourless. It strains my mind to separate colour and sound from objects. Since my education began I have always had things described to me with their colours and sounds by one with keen senses and a fine feeling for the significant. Therefore I habitually think of things as coloured and resonant. Habit accounts for part. The soul sense accounts for another part. The brain with its five-sensed construction asserts its right and accounts for the rest. Inclusive of all, the unity of the world demands that colour be kept in it, whether I have cognizance of it or not. Rather than be shut out, I take part in it by discussing it, imagining it, happy in the happiness of those near me who gaze at the lovely hues of the sunset or the rainbow.

My hand has its share in this multiple knowledge, but it must never be forgotten that with the fingers I see only a very small portion of a surface, and that I must pass my hand continually over it before my touch grasps the whole. It is still more important, however, to remember that my imagination is not tethered to certain points, locations, and distances. It puts all the parts together simultaneously as if it saw or knew instead of feeling them. Though I feel only a small part of my horse at a time,—my horse is nervous and does not submit to manual explorations,—yet, because I have many times felt hock, nose, hoof and mane, I can see the steeds of Phœbus Apollo coursing the heavens.

With such a power active it is impossible that my thought should be vague, indistinct. It must needs be potent, definite. This is really a corollary of the philosophical truth that the real world exists only for the mind. That is to say, I can never touch the world in its entirety; indeed, I touch less of it than the portion that others see or hear. But all creatures, all objects, pass into my brain entire, and occupy the same extent there that they do in material space. I declare that for me branched thoughts, instead of pines, wave, sway, rustle, make musical the ridges of mountains rising summit upon summit. Mention a rose too far away for me to smell it. Straightway a scent steals into my nostril, a form presses against my palm in all its dilating softness, with rounded petals, slightly curled edges, curving stem, leaves drooping. When I would fain view the world as a whole, it rushes into vision—man, beast, bird, reptile, fly, sky, ocean, mountains, plain, rock, pebble. The warmth of life, the reality of creation is over all—the throb of human hands, glossiness of fur, lithe windings of long bodies, poignant buzzing of insects, the ruggedness of the steeps as I climb them, the liquid mobility and boom of waves upon the rocks. Strange to say, try as I may, I cannot force my touch to pervade this universe in all directions. The moment I try, the whole vanishes; only small objects or narrow portions of a surface, mere touch-signs, a chaos of things scattered at random, remain. No thrill, no delight is excited thereby. Restore to the artistic, comprehensive internal sense its rightful domain, and you give me joy which best proves the reality.

XI
BEFORE THE SOUL DAWN

BEFORE MY teacher came to me, I did not know that I am. I lived in a world that was a no-world. I cannot hope to describe adequately that unconscious, yet conscious time of nothingness. I did not know that I knew aught, or that I lived or acted or desired. I had neither will nor intellect. I was carried along to objects and acts by a certain blind natural impetus. I had a mind which caused me to feel anger, satisfaction, desire. These two facts led those about me to suppose that I willed and thought. I can remember all this, not because I knew that it was so, but because I have tactual memory. It enables me to remember that I never contracted my forehead in the act of thinking. I never viewed anything beforehand or chose it. I also recall tactually the fact that never in a start of the body or a heart-beat did I feel that I loved or cared for anything. My inner life, then, was a blank without past, present, or future, without hope or anticipation, without wonder or joy or faith.

> *It was not night—it was not day.*
> . . . . .
> *But vacancy absorbing space,*
> *And fixedness, without a place;*
> *There were no stars—no earth—no time—*
> *No check—no change—no good—no crime.*

My dormant being had no idea of God or immortality, no fear of death.

I remember, also through touch, that I had a power of association. I felt tactual jars like the stamp of a foot, the opening of a window or its closing, the slam of a door. After repeatedly smelling rain and feeling the discomfort of wetness, I acted like those about me: I ran to shut the window. But that was not thought in any sense. It was the same kind of association that makes animals take shelter from the rain. From the same instinct of aping others, I folded the clothes that came from the laundry, and put mine away, fed the turkeys, sewed bead-eyes on my doll's face, and did many other things of which I have the tactual remembrance.

When I wanted anything I liked,—ice-cream, for instance, of which I was very fond,—I had a delicious taste on my tongue (which, by the way, I never have now), and in my hand I felt the turning of the freezer. I made the sign, and my mother knew I wanted ice-cream. I "thought" and desired in my fingers. If I had made a man, I should certainly have put the brain and soul in his finger-tips. From reminiscences like these I conclude that it is the opening of the two faculties, freedom of will, or choice, and rationality, or the power of thinking from one thing to another, which makes it possible to come into being first as a child, afterwards as a man.

Since I had no power of thought, I did not compare one mental state with another. So I was not conscious of any change or process going on in my brain when my teacher began to instruct me. I merely felt keen delight in obtaining more easily what I wanted by means of the finger motions she taught me. I thought only of objects, and only objects I wanted. It was the turning of the freezer on a larger scale. When I learned the meaning of "I" and "me" and found that I was something, I began to think. Then consciousness first existed for me. Thus it was not the sense of touch that brought me knowledge. It was the awakening of my soul that first rendered my senses their value, their cognizance of objects, names, qualities, and properties. Thought made me conscious of love, joy, and all the emotions. I was eager to know, then to understand, afterward to reflect on what I knew and understood, and the blind impetus, which had before driven me hither and thither at the dictates of my sensations, vanished forever.

I cannot represent more clearly than any one else the gradual and subtle changes from first impressions to abstract ideas. But I know that my physical ideas, that is, ideas derived from material objects, appear to me first an idea similar to those of touch. Instantly they pass into intellectual meanings. Afterward the meaning finds expression in what is called "inner speech." When I was a child, my inner speech was inner spelling. Although I am even now frequently caught spelling to myself on my fingers, yet I talk to myself, too, with my lips, and it is true that when I first learned to speak, my mind discarded the finger-symbols and began to articulate. However, when I try to recall what some one has said to me, I am conscious of a hand spelling into mine.

It has often been asked what were my earliest impressions of the world in which I found myself. But one who thinks at all of his first impressions knows what a riddle this is. Our impressions grow and change unnoticed, so that what we suppose we thought as children may be quite different from what we actually experienced in our childhood. I only know that after my education began the world which came within my reach was all alive. I spelled to my blocks and my dogs. I sympathized with plants when the flowers were picked, because I thought it hurt them, and that they grieved for their lost blossoms. It was two years before I could be made to believe that my dogs did not understand what I said, and I always apologized to them when I ran into or stepped on them.

As my experiences broadened and deepened, the indeterminate, poetic feelings of childhood began to fix themselves in definite thoughts. Nature—the world I could touch—was folded and filled with myself. I am inclined to believe those philosophers who declare that we know nothing but our own feelings and ideas. With a little ingenious reasoning one may see in the material world simply a mirror, an image of permanent mental sensations. In either sphere self-knowledge is the condition and the limit of our consciousness. That is why, perhaps, many people know so little about what is beyond their short range of experience. They look within themselves—and find nothing! Therefore they conclude that there is nothing outside themselves, either.

However that may be, I came later to look for an image of my emotions and sensations in others. I had to learn the outward signs of inward feelings. The start of fear, the suppressed, controlled tensity of pain, the beat of happy muscles in others, had to be perceived and compared with my own experiences before I could trace them back to the intangible soul of another. Groping, uncertain, I at last found my identity, and after seeing my thoughts and feelings repeated in others, I gradually constructed my world of men and of God. As I read and study, I find that this is what the rest of the race has done. Man looks within himself and in time finds the measure and the meaning of the universe.

XII
THE LARGER SANCTIONS

SO, IN the midst of life, eager, imperious life, the deaf-blind child, fettered to the bare rock of circumstance, spider-like, sends out gossamer threads of thought into the measureless void that surrounds him. Patiently he explores the dark, until he builds up a knowledge of the world he lives in, and his soul meets the beauty of the world, where the sun shines always, and the birds sing. To the blind child the dark is kindly. In it he finds nothing extraordinary or terrible. It is his familiar world; even the groping from place to place, the halting steps, the dependence upon others, do not seem strange to him. He does not know how many countless pleasures the dark shuts out from him. Not until he weighs his life in the scale of others' experience does he realize what it is to live forever in the dark. But the knowledge that teaches him this bitterness also brings its consolation—spiritual light, the promise of the day that shall be.

The blind child—the deaf-blind child—has inherited the mind of seeing and hearing ancestors—a mind measured to five senses. Therefore he must be influenced, even if it be unknown to himself, by the light, colour, song which have been transmitted through the language he is taught, for the chambers of the mind are ready to receive that language. The brain of the race is so permeated with colour that it dyes even the speech of the blind. Every object I think of is stained with the hue that belongs to it by association and memory. The experience of the deaf-blind person, in a world of seeing, hearing people, is like that of a sailor on an island where the inhabitants speak a language unknown to him, whose life is unlike that he has lived. He is one, they are many; there is no chance of compromise. He must learn to see with their eyes, to hear with their ears, to think their thoughts, to follow their ideals.

If the dark, silent world which surrounds him were essentially different from the sunlit, resonant world, it would be incomprehensible to his kind, and could never be discussed. If his feelings and sensations were fundamentally different from those of others, they would be inconceivable except to those who had similar sensations and feelings. If the mental consciousness of the deaf-blind person were absolutely dissimilar to that of his fellows, he would have no means of imagining what they think. Since the mind of the sightless is essentially the same as that of the seeing in that it admits of no lack, it must supply some sort of equivalent for missing physical sensations. It must perceive a likeness between things outward and things inward, a correspondence between the seen and the unseen. I make use of such a correspondence in many relations, and no matter how far I pursue it to things I cannot see, it does not break under the test.

As a working hypothesis, correspondence is adequate to all life, through the whole range of phenomena. The flash of thought and its swiftness explain the lightning flash and the sweep of a comet through the heavens. My mental sky opens to me the vast celestial spaces, and I proceed to fill them with the images of my spiritual stars. I recognize truth by the clearness and guidance that it gives my thought, and, knowing what that clearness is, I can imagine what light is to the eye. It is not a convention of language, but a forcible feeling of the reality, that at times makes me start when I say, "Oh, I see my mistake!" or "How dark, cheerless is his life!" I know these are metaphors. Still, I must prove with them, since there is nothing in our language to replace them. Deaf-blind metaphors to correspond do not exist and are not necessary. Because I can understand the word "reflect" figuratively, a mirror has never perplexed me. The manner in which my imagination perceives absent things enables me to see how glasses can magnify things, bring them nearer, or remove them farther.

Deny me this correspondence, this internal sense, confine me to the fragmentary, incoherent touch-world, and lo, I become as a bat which wanders about on the wing. Suppose I omitted all words of seeing, hearing, colour, light, landscape, the thousand phenomena, instruments and beauties connected with them. I should suffer a great diminution of the wonder and delight in attaining knowledge; also—more dreadful loss—my emotions would be blunted, so that I could not be touched by things unseen.

Has anything arisen to disprove the adequacy of correspondence? Has any chamber of the blind man's brain been opened and found empty? Has any psychologist explored the mind of the sightless and been able to say, "There is no sensation here"?

I tread the solid earth; I breathe the scented air. Out of these two experiences I form numberless associations and correspondences. I observe, I feel, I think, I imagine. I associate the countless varied impressions, experiences, concepts. Out of these materials Fancy, the cunning artisan of the brain, welds an image which the sceptic would deny me, because I cannot see with my physical eyes the changeful, lovely face of my thought-child. He would break the mind's mirror. This spirit-vandal would humble my soul and force me to bite the dust of material things. While I champ the bit of circumstance, he scourges and goads me with the spur of fact. If I heeded him, the sweet-visaged earth would vanish into nothing, and I should hold in my hand nought but an aimless, soulless lump of dead matter. But although the body physical is rooted alive to the Promethean rock, the spirit-proud huntress of the air will still pursue the shining, open highways of the universe.

Blindness has no limiting effect upon mental vision. My intellectual horizon is infinitely wide. The universe it encircles is immeasurable. Would they who bid me keep within the narrow bound of my meagre senses demand of Herschel that he roof his stellar universe and give us back Plato's solid firmament of glassy spheres? Would they command Darwin from the grave and bid him blot out his geological time, give us back a paltry few thousand years? Oh, the supercilious doubters! They ever strive to clip the upward daring wings of the spirit.

A person deprived of one or more senses is not, as many seem to think, turned out into a trackless wilderness without landmark or guide. The blind man carries with him into his dark environment all the faculties essential to the apprehension of the visible world whose door is closed behind him. He finds his surroundings everywhere homogeneous with those of the sunlit world; for there is an inexhaustible ocean of likenesses between the world within, and the world without, and these likenesses, these correspondences, he finds equal to every exigency his life offers.

The necessity of some such thing as correspondence or symbolism appears more and more urgent as we consider the duties that religion and philosophy enjoin upon us.

The blind are expected to read the Bible as a means of attaining spiritual happiness. Now, the Bible is filled throughout with references to clouds, stars, colours, and beauty, and often the mention of these is essential to the meaning of the parable or the message in which they occur. Here one must needs see the inconsistency of people who believe in the Bible, and yet deny us a right to talk about what we do not see, and for that matter what *they* do not see, either. Who shall forbid my heart to sing: "Yea, he did fly upon the wings of the wind. He made darkness his secret place; his pavilion round about him were dark waters and thick clouds of the skies"?

Philosophy constantly points out the untrustworthiness of the five senses and the important work of reason which corrects the errors of sight and reveals its illusions. If we cannot depend on five senses, how much less may we rely on three! What ground have we for discarding light, sound, and colour as an integral part of our world? How are we to know that they have ceased to exist for us? We must take their reality for granted, even as the philosopher assumes the reality of the world without being able to see it physically as a whole.

Ancient philosophy offers an argument which seems still valid. There is in the blind as in the seeing an Absolute which gives truth to what we know to be true, order to what is orderly, beauty to the beautiful, touchableness to what is tangible. If this is granted, it follows that this Absolute is not imperfect, incomplete, partial. It must needs go beyond the limited evidence of our sensations, and also give light to what is invisible, music to the musical that silence dulls. Thus mind itself compels us to acknowledge that we are in a world of intellectual order, beauty, and harmony. The essences, or absolutes of these ideas, necessarily dispel their opposites which belong with evil, disorder and discord. Thus deafness and blindness do not exist in the immaterial mind, which is philosophically the real world, but are banished with the perishable material senses. Reality, of which visible things are the symbol, shines before my mind. While I walk about my chamber with unsteady steps, my spirit sweeps skyward on eagle wings and looks out with unquenchable vision upon the world of eternal beauty.

XIII
THE DREAM WORLD

EVERYBODY TAKES his own dreams seriously, but yawns at the breakfast-table when somebody else begins to tell the adventures of the night before. I hesitate, therefore, to enter upon an account of my dreams; for it is a literary sin to bore the reader, and a scientific sin to report the facts of a far country with more regard to point and brevity than to complete and literal truth. The psychologists have trained a pack of theories and facts which they keep in leash, like so many bulldogs, and which they let loose upon us whenever we depart from the straight and narrow path of dream probability. One may not even tell an entertaining dream without being suspected of having liberally edited it,—as if editing were one of the seven deadly sins, instead of a useful and honourable occupation! Be it understood, then, that I am discoursing at my own breakfast-table, and that no scientific man is present to trip the autocrat.

I used to wonder why scientific men and others were always asking me about my dreams. But I am not surprised now, since I have discovered what some of them believe to be the ordinary waking experience of one who is both deaf and blind. They think that I can know very little about objects even a few feet beyond the reach of my arms. Everything outside of myself, according to them, is a hazy blur. Trees, mountains, cities, the ocean, even the house I live in are but fairy fabrications, misty unrealities. Therefore it is assumed that my dreams should have peculiar interest for the man of science. In some undefined way it is expected that they should reveal the world I dwell in to be flat, formless, colourless, without perspective, with little thickness and less solidity—a vast solitude of soundless space. But who shall put into words limitless, visionless, silent void? One should be a disembodied spirit indeed to make anything out of such insubstantial experiences. A world, or a dream for that matter, to be comprehensible to us, must, I should think, have a warp of substance woven into the woof of fantasy. We cannot imagine even in dreams an object which has no counterpart in reality. Ghosts always resemble somebody, and if they do not appear themselves, their presence is indicated by circumstances with which we are perfectly familiar.

During sleep we enter a strange, mysterious realm which science has thus far not explored. Beyond the border-line of slumber the investigator may not pass with his common-sense rule and test. Sleep with softest touch locks all the gates of our physical senses and lulls to rest the conscious will—the disciplinarian of our waking thoughts. Then the spirit wrenches itself free from the sinewy arms of reason and like a winged courser spurns the firm green earth and speeds away upon wind and cloud, leaving neither trace nor footprint by which science may track its flight and bring us knowledge of the distant, shadowy country that we nightly visit. When we come back from the dream-realm, we can give no reasonable report of what we met there. But once across the border, we feel at home as if we had always lived there and had never made any excursions into this rational daylight world.

My dreams do not seem to differ very much from the dreams of other people. Some of them are coherent and safely hitched to an event or a conclusion. Others are inconsequent and fantastic. All attest that in Dreamland there is no such thing as repose. We are always up and doing with a mind for any adventure. We act, strive, think, suffer and are glad to no purpose. We leave outside the portals of Sleep all troublesome incredulities and vexatious speculations as to probability. I float wraith-like upon clouds in and out among the winds, without the faintest notion that I am doing anything unusual. In Dreamland I find little that is altogether strange or wholly new to my experience. No matter what happens, I am not astonished, however extraordinary the circumstances may be. I visit a foreign land where I have not been in reality, and I converse with peoples whose language I have never heard. Yet we manage to understand each other perfectly. Into whatsoever situation or society my wanderings bring me, there is the same homogeneity. If I happen into Vagabondia, I make merry with the jolly folk of the road or the tavern.

I do not remember ever to have met persons with whom I could not at once communicate, or to have been shocked or surprised at the doings of my dream-companions. In its strange wanderings in those dusky groves of Slumberland my soul takes everything for granted and adapts itself to the wildest phantoms. I am seldom confused. Everything is as clear as day. I know events the instant they take place, and wherever I turn my steps, Mind is my faithful guide and interpreter.

I suppose every one has had in a dream the exasperating, profitless experience of seeking something urgently desired at the moment, and the aching, weary sensation that follows each failure to track the thing to its hiding-place. Sometimes with a singing dizziness in my head I climb and climb, I know not where or why. Yet I cannot quit the torturing, passionate endeavour, though again and again I reach out blindly for an object to hold to. Of course according to the perversity of dreams there is no object near. I clutch empty air, and then I fall downward, and still downward, and in the midst of the fall I dissolve into the atmosphere upon which I have been floating so precariously.

Some of my dreams seem to be traced one within another like a series of concentric circles. In sleep I think I cannot sleep. I toss about in the toils of tasks unfinished. I decide to get up and read for a while. I know the shelf in my library where I keep the book I want. The book has no name, but I find it without difficulty. I settle myself comfortably in the morris-chair, the great book open on my knee. Not a word can I make out, the pages are utterly blank. I am not surprised, but keenly disappointed. I finger the pages, I bend over them lovingly, the tears fall on my hands. I shut the book quickly as the thought passes through my mind, "The print will be all rubbed out if I get it wet." Yet there is no print tangible on the page!

This morning I thought that I awoke. I was certain that I had overslept. I seized my watch, and sure enough, it pointed to an hour after my rising time. I sprang up in the greatest hurry, knowing that breakfast was ready. I called my mother, who declared that my watch must be wrong. She was positive it could not be so late. I looked at my watch again, and lo! the hands wiggled, whirled, buzzed and disappeared. I awoke more fully as my dismay grew, until I was at the antipodes of sleep. Finally my eyes opened actually, and I knew that I had been dreaming. I had only waked into sleep. What is still more bewildering, there is no difference between the consciousness of the sham waking and that of the real one.

It is fearful to think that all that we have ever seen, felt, read, and done may suddenly rise to our dream-vision, as the sea casts up objects it has swallowed. I have held a little child in my arms in the midst of a riot and spoken vehemently, imploring the Russian soldiers not to massacre the Jews. I have re-lived the agonizing scenes of the Sepoy Rebellion and the French Revolution. Cities have burned before my eyes, and I have fought the flames until I fell exhausted. Holocausts overtake the world, and I struggle in vain to save my friends.

Once in a dream a message came speeding over land and sea that winter was descending upon the world from the North Pole, that the Arctic zone was shifting to our mild climate. Far and wide the message flew. The ocean was congealed in midsummer. Ships were held fast in the ice by thousands, the ships with large, white sails were held fast. Riches of the Orient and the plenteous harvests of the Golden West might no more pass between nation and nation. For some time the trees and flowers grew on, despite the intense cold. Birds flew into the houses for safety, and those which winter had overtaken lay on the snow with wings spread in vain flight. At last the foliage and blossoms fell at the feet of Winter. The petals of the flowers were turned to rubies and sapphires.

The leaves froze into emeralds. The trees moaned and tossed their branches as the frost pierced them through bark and sap, pierced into their very roots. I shivered myself awake, and with a tumult of joy I breathed the many sweet morning odours wakened by the summer sun.

One need not visit an African jungle or an Indian forest to hunt the tiger. One can lie in bed amid downy pillows and dream tigers as terrible as any in the pathless wild. I was a little girl when one night I tried to cross the garden in front of my aunt's house in Alabama. I was in pursuit of a large cat with a great bushy tail. A few hours before he had clawed my little canary out of its cage and crunched it between his cruel teeth. I could not see the cat. But the thought in my mind was distinct: "He is making for the high grass at the end of the garden. I'll get there first!" I put my hand on the box border and ran swiftly along the path. When I reached the high grass, there was the cat gliding into the wavy tangle. I rushed forward and tried to seize him and take the bird from between his teeth. To my horror a huge beast, not the cat at all, sprang out from the grass, and his sinewy shoulder rubbed against me with palpitating strength! His ears stood up and quivered with anger. His eyes were hot. His nostrils were large and wet. His lips moved horribly. I knew it was a tiger, a real live tiger, and that I should be devoured—my little bird and I. I do not know what happened after that. The next important thing seldom happens in dreams.

Some time earlier I had a dream which made a vivid impression upon me. My aunt was weeping because she could not find me. But I took an impish pleasure in the thought that she and others were searching for me, and making great noise which I felt through my feet. Suddenly the spirit of mischief gave way to uncertainty and fear. I felt cold. The air smelt like ice and salt. I tried to run; but the long grass tripped me, and I fell forward on my face. I lay very still, feeling with all my body. After a while my sensations seemed to be concentrated in my fingers, and I perceived that the grass blades were sharp as knives, and hurt my hands cruelly. I tried to get up cautiously, so as not to cut myself on the sharp grass. I put down a tentative foot, much as my kitten treads for the first time the primeval forest in the backyard. All at once I felt the stealthy patter of something creeping, creeping, creeping purposefully toward me. I do not know how at that time the idea was in my mind; I had no words for intention or purpose. Yet it was precisely the evil intent, and not the creeping animal that terrified me. I had no fear of living creatures. I loved my father's dogs, the frisky little calf, the gentle cows, the horses and mules that ate apples from my hand, and none of them had ever harmed me. I lay low, waiting in breathless terror for the creature to spring and bury its long claws in my flesh. I thought, "They will feel like turkey-claws." Something warm and wet touched my face. I shrieked, struck out frantically, and awoke. Something was still struggling in my arms. I held on with might and main until I was exhausted, then I loosed my hold. I found dear old Belle, the setter, shaking herself and looking at me reproachfully. She and I had gone to sleep together on the rug, and had naturally wandered to the dream-forest where dogs and little girls hunt wild game and have strange adventures. We encountered hosts of elfin foes, and it required all the dog tactics at Belle's command to acquit herself like the lady and huntress that she was. Belle had her dreams too. We used to lie under the trees and flowers in the old garden, and I used to laugh with delight when the magnolia leaves fell with little thuds, and Belle jumped up, thinking she had heard a partridge. She would pursue the leaf, point it, bring it back to me and lay it at my feet with a humorous wag of her tail as much as to say, "This is the kind of bird that waked me." I made a chain for her neck out of the lovely blue Paulownia flowers and covered her with great heart-shaped leaves.

Dear old Belle, she has long been dreaming among the lotus-flowers and poppies of the dogs' paradise.

Certain dreams have haunted me since my childhood. One which recurs often proceeds after this wise: A spirit seems to pass before my face. I feel an extreme heat like the blast from an engine. It is the embodiment of evil. I must have had it first after the day that I nearly got burnt.

Another spirit which visits me often brings a sensation of cool dampness, such as one feels on a chill November night when the window is open. The spirit stops just beyond my reach, sways back and forth like a creature in grief. My blood is chilled, and seems to freeze in my veins. I try to move, but my body is still, and I cannot even cry out. After a while the spirit passes on, and I say to myself shudderingly, "That was Death. I wonder if he has taken her." The pronoun stands for my Teacher.

In my dreams I have sensations, odours, tastes and ideas which I do not remember to have had in reality. Perhaps they are the glimpses which my mind catches through the veil of sleep of my earliest babyhood. I have heard "the trampling of many waters." Sometimes a wonderful light visits me in sleep. Such a flash and glory as it is! I gaze and gaze until it vanishes. I smell and taste much as in my waking hours; but the sense of touch plays a less important part. In sleep I almost never grope. No one guides me. Even in a crowded street I am self-sufficient, and I enjoy an independence quite foreign to my physical life. Now I seldom spell on my fingers, and it is still rarer for others to spell into my hand. My mind acts independent of my physical organs. I am delighted to be thus endowed, if only in sleep; for then my soul dons its winged sandals and joyfully joins the throng of happy beings who dwell beyond the reaches of bodily sense.

The moral inconsistency of dreams is glaring. Mine grow less and less accordant with my proper principles. I am nightly hurled into an unethical medley of extremes. I must either defend another to the last drop of my blood or condemn him past all repenting. I commit murder, sleeping, to save the lives of others. I ascribe to those I love best acts and words which it mortifies me to remember, and I cast reproach after reproach upon them. It is fortunate for our peace of mind that most wicked dreams are soon forgotten. Death, sudden and awful, strange loves and hates remorselessly pursued, cunningly plotted revenge, are seldom more than dim haunting recollections in the morning, and during the day they are erased by the normal activities of the mind. Sometimes immediately on waking, I am so vexed at the memory of a dream-fracas, I wish I may dream no more. With this wish distinctly before me I drop off again into a new turmoil of dreams.

Oh, dreams, what opprobrium I heap upon you—you, the most pointless things imaginable, saucy apes, brewers of odious contrasts, haunting birds of ill omen, mocking echoes, unseasonable reminders, oft-returning vexations, skeletons in my morris-chair, jesters in the tomb, death's-heads at the wedding feast, outlaws of the brain that every night defy the mind's police service, thieves of my Hesperidean apples, breakers of my domestic peace, murderers of sleep. "Oh, dreadful dreams that do fright my spirit from her propriety!" No wonder that Hamlet preferred the ills he knew rather than run the risk of one dream-vision.

Yet remove the dream-world, and the loss is inconceivable. The magic spell which binds poetry together is broken. The splendour of art and the soaring might of imagination are lessened because no phantom of fadeless sunsets and flowers urges onward to a goal. Gone is the mute permission or connivance which emboldens the soul to mock the limits of time and space, forecast and gather in harvests of achievement for ages yet unborn. Blot out dreams, and the blind lose one of their chief comforts; for in the visions of sleep they behold their belief in the seeing mind and their expectation of light beyond the blank, narrow night justified. Nay, our conception of immortality is shaken. Faith, the motive-power of human life, flickers out. Before such vacancy and bareness the shocks of wrecked worlds were indeed welcome. In truth, dreams bring us the thought independently of us and in spite of us that the soul

> "may right
> Her nature, shoot large sail on lengthening cord,
> And rush exultant on the Infinite."

XIV
DREAMS AND REALITY

IT IS ASTONISHING to think how our real wide-awake world revolves around the shadowy unrealities of Dreamland. Despite all that we say about the inconsequence of dreams, we often reason by them. We stake our greatest hopes upon them. Nay, we build upon them the fabric of an ideal world. I can recall few fine, thoughtful poems, few noble works of art or any system of philosophy in which there is not evidence that dream-fantasies symbolize truths concealed by phenomena.

The fact that in dreams confusion reigns, and illogical connections occur gives plausibility to the theory which Sir Arthur Mitchell and other scientific men hold, that our dream-thinking is uncontrolled and undirected by the will. The will—the inhibiting and guiding power—finds rest and refreshment in sleep, while the mind, like a barque without rudder or compass, drifts aimlessly upon an uncharted sea. But curiously enough, these fantasies and inter-twistings of thought are to be found in great imaginative poems like Spenser's "Færie Queene." Lamb was impressed by the analogy between our dream-thinking and the work of the imagination. Speaking of the episode in the cave of Mammon, Lamb wrote:

"It is not enough to say that the whole episode is a copy of the mind's conceptions in sleep; it is—in some sort, but what a copy! Let the most romantic of us that has been entertained all night with the spectacle of some wild and magnificent vision, re-combine it in the morning and try it by his waking judgment. That which appeared so shifting and yet so coherent, when it came under cool examination, shall appear so reasonless and so unlinked, that we are ashamed to have been so deluded, and to have taken, though but in sleep, a monster for a god. The transitions in this episode are every whit as violent as in the most extravagant dream, and yet the waking judgment ratifies them."

Perhaps I feel more than others the analogy between the world of our waking life and the world of dreams because before I was taught, I lived in a sort of perpetual dream. The testimony of parents and friends who watched me day after day is the only means that I have of knowing the actuality of those early, obscure years of my childhood. The physical acts of going to bed and waking in the morning alone mark the transition from reality to Dreamland. As near as I can tell, asleep or awake I only felt with my body. I can recollect no process which I should now dignify with the term of thought. It is true that my bodily sensations were extremely acute; but beyond a crude connection with physical wants they are not associated or directed. They had little relation to each other, to me or the experience of others. Idea—that which gives identity and continuity to experience—came into my sleeping and waking existence at the same moment with the awakening of self-consciousness. Before that moment my mind was in a state of anarchy in which meaningless sensations rioted, and if thought existed, it was so vague and inconsequent, it cannot be made a part of discourse. Yet before my education began, I dreamed. I know that I must have dreamed because I recall no break in my tactual experiences. Things fell suddenly, heavily. I felt my clothing afire, or I fell into a tub of cold water. Once I smelt bananas, and the odour in my nostrils was so vivid that in the morning, before I was dressed, I went to the sideboard to look for the bananas. There were no bananas, and no odour of bananas anywhere! My life was in fact a dream throughout.

The likeness between my waking state and the sleeping one is still marked. In both states I see, but not with my eyes. I hear, but not with my ears. I speak, and am spoken to, without the sound of a voice. I am moved to pleasure by visions of ineffable beauty which I have never beheld in the physical world. Once in a dream I held in my hand a pearl. The one I saw in my dreams must, therefore, have been a creation of my imagination. It was a smooth, exquisitely moulded crystal. As I gazed into its shimmering deeps, my soul was flooded with an ecstasy of tenderness, and I was filled with wonder as one who should for the first time look into the cool, sweet heart of a rose. My pearl was dew and fire, the velvety green of moss, the soft whiteness of lilies, and the distilled hues and sweetness of a thousand roses. It seemed to me, the soul of beauty was dissolved in its crystal bosom. This beauteous vision strengthens my conviction that the world which the mind builds up out of countless subtle experiences and suggestions is fairer than the world of the senses. The splendour of the sunset my friends gaze at across the purpling hills is wonderful. But the sunset of the inner vision brings purer delight because it is the worshipful blending of all the beauty that we have known and desired.

I believe that I am more fortunate in my dreams than most people; for as I think back over my dreams, the pleasant ones seem to predominate, although we naturally recall most vividly and tell most eagerly the grotesque and fantastic adventures in Slumberland. I have friends, however, whose dreams are always troubled and disturbed. They wake fatigued and bruised, and they tell me that they would give a kingdom for one dreamless night. There is one friend who declares that she has never had a felicitous dream in her life. The grind and worry of the day invade the sweet domain of sleep and weary her with incessant, profitless effort. I feel very sorry for this friend, and perhaps it is hardly fair to insist upon the pleasure of dreaming in the presence of one whose dream-experience is so unhappy. Still, it is true that my dreams have uses as many and sweet as those of adversity. All my yearning for the strange, the weird, the ghostlike is gratified in dreams. They carry me out of the accustomed and commonplace. In a flash, in the winking of an eye they snatch the burden from my shoulder, the trivial task from my hand and the pain and disappointment from my heart, and I behold the lovely face of my dream. It dances round me with merry measure and darts hither and thither in happy abandon. Sudden, sweet fancies spring forth from every nook and corner, and delightful surprises meet me at every turn. A happy dream is more precious than gold and rubies.

I like to think that in dreams we catch glimpses of a life larger than our own. We see it as a little child, or as a savage who visits a civilized nation. Thoughts are imparted to us far above our ordinary thinking. Feelings nobler and wiser than any we have known thrill us between heart-beats. For one fleeting night a princelier nature captures us, and we become as great as our aspirations. I daresay we return to the little world of our daily activities with as distorted a half-memory of what we have seen as that of the African who visited England, and afterwards said he had been in a huge hill which carried him over great waters. The comprehensiveness of our thought, whether we are asleep or awake, no doubt depends largely upon our idiosyncrasies, constitution, habits, and mental capacity. But whatever may be the nature of our dreams, the mental processes that characterize them are analogous to those which go on when the mind is not held to attention by the will.

XV
A WAKING DREAM

I HAVE sat for hours in a sort of reverie, letting my mind have its way without inhibition and direction, and idly noted down the incessant beat of thought upon thought, image upon image. I have observed that my thoughts make all kinds of connections, wind in and out, trace concentric circles, and break up in eddies of fantasy, just as in dreams. One day I had a literary frolic with a certain set of thoughts which dropped in for an afternoon call. I wrote for three or four hours as they arrived, and the resulting record is much[2] like a dream. I found that the most disconnected, dissimilar thoughts came in arm-in-arm—I dreamed a wide-awake dream. The difference is that in waking dreams I can look back upon the endless succession of thoughts, while in the dreams of sleep I can recall but few ideas and images. I catch broken threads from the warp and woof of a pattern I cannot see, or glowing leaves which have floated on a slumber-wind from a tree that I cannot identify. In this reverie I held the key to the company of ideas. I give my record of them to show what analogies exist between thoughts when they are not directed and the behaviour of real dream-thinking.

I had an essay to write. I wanted my mind fresh and obedient, and all its handmaidens ready to hold up my hands in the task. I intended to discourse learnedly upon my educational experiences, and I was unusually anxious to do my best. I had a working plan in my head for the essay, which was to be grave, wise, and abounding in ideas. Moreover, it was to have an academic flavour suggestive of sheepskin, and the reader was to be duly impressed with the austere dignity of cap and gown. I shut myself up in the study, resolved to beat out on the keys of my typewriter this immortal chapter of my life-history. Alexander was no more confident of conquering Asia with the splendid army which his father Philip had disciplined than I was of finding my mental house in order and my thoughts obedient. My mind had had a long vacation, and I was now coming back to it in an hour that it looked not for me. My situation was similar to that of the master who went into a far country and expected on his home coming to find everything as he left it. But returning he found his servants giving a party. Confusion was rampant. There was fiddling and dancing and the babble of many tongues, so that the voice of the master could not be heard. Though he shouted and beat upon the gate, it remained closed.

So it was with me. I sounded the trumpet loud and long; but the vassals of thought would not rally to my standard. Each had his arm round the waist of a fair partner, and I know not what wild tunes "put life and mettle into their heels." There was nothing to do. I looked about helplessly upon my great retinue, and realized that it is not the possession of a thing but the ability to use it which is of value. I settled back in my chair to watch the pageant. It was rather pleasant sitting there, "idle as a painted ship upon a painted ocean," watching my own thoughts at play. It was like thinking fine things to say without taking the trouble to write them. I felt like Alice in Wonderland when she ran at full speed with the red queen and never passed anything or got anywhere.

The merry frolic went on madly. The dancers were all manner of thoughts. There were sad thoughts and happy thoughts, thoughts suited to every clime and weather, thoughts bearing the mark of every age and nation, silly thoughts and wise thoughts, thoughts of people, of things, and of nothing, good thoughts, impish thoughts, and large, gracious thoughts. There they went swinging hand-in-hand in corkscrew fashion. An antic jester in green and gold led the dance. The guests followed no order or precedent. No two thoughts were related to each other even by the fortieth cousinship. There was not so much as an international alliance between them. Each thought behaved like a newly created poet.

> "His mouth he could not ope,
> But there flew out a trope."

Magical lyrics—oh, if I only had written them down! Pell-mell they came down the sequestered avenues of my mind, this merry throng. With bacchanal song and shout they came, and eye hath not since beheld confusion worse confounded.

Shut your eyes, and see them come—the knights and ladies of my revel. Plumed and turbaned they come, clad in mail and silken broideries, gentle maids in Quaker gray, gay princes in scarlet cloaks, coquettes with roses in their hair, monks in cowls that might have covered the tall Minster Tower, demure little girls hugging paper dolls, and rollicking school-boys with ruddy morning faces, an absent-minded professor carrying his shoes under his arms and looking wise, followed by cronies, fairies, goblins, and all the troops just loosed from Noah's storm-tossed ark. They walked, they strutted, they soared, they swam, and some came in through fire. One sprite climbed up to the moon on a ladder made of leaves and frozen dew-drops. A peacock with a great hooked bill flew in and out among the branches of a pomegranate-tree pecking the rosy fruit. He screamed so loud that Apollo turned in his chariot of flame and from his burnished bow shot golden arrows at him. This did not disturb the peacock in the least; for he spread his gem-like wings and flourished his wonderful, fire-tipped tail in the very face of the sun-god! Then came Venus—an exact copy of my own plaster cast—serene, calm-eyed, dancing "high and disposedly" like Queen Elizabeth, surrounded by a troop of lovely Cupids mounted on rose-tinted clouds, blown hither and thither by sweet winds, while all around danced flowers and streams and queer little Japanese cherry-trees in pots! They were followed by jovial Pan with green hair and jewelled sandals, and by his side—I could scarcely believe my eyes!—walked a modest nun counting her beads. At a little distance were seen three dancers arm-in-arm, a lean, starved platitude, a rosy, dimpled joke, and a steel-ribbed sermon on predestination. Close upon them came a whole string of Nights with wind-blown hair and Days with faggots on their backs. All at once I saw the ample figure of Life rise above the whirling mass holding a naked child in one hand and in the other a gleaming sword. A bear crouched at her feet, and all about her swirled and glowed a multitudinous host of tiny atoms which sang all together, "We are the will of God." Atom wedded atom, and chemical married chemical, and the cosmic dance went on in changing, changeless measure, until my head sang like a buzz-saw.

Just as I was thinking I would leave this scene of phantoms and take a stroll in the quiet groves of Slumber I noticed a commotion near one of the entrances to my enchanted palace. It was evident from the whispering and buzzing that went round that more celebrities had arrived. The first personage I saw was Homer, blind no more, leading by a golden chain the white-beaked ships of the Achaians bobbing their heads and squawking like so many white swans. Plato and Mother Goose with the numerous children of the shoe came next. Simple Simon, Jill, and Jack who had had his head mended, and the cat that fell into the cream—all these danced in a giddy reel, while Plato solemnly discoursed on the laws of Topsyturvy Land. Then followed grim-visaged Calvin and "violet-crowned, sweet-smiling Sappho" who danced a Schottische. Aristophanes and Molière joined for a measure, both talking at once, Molière in Greek and Aristophanes in German. I thought this odd, because it occurred to me that German was a dead language before Aristophanes was born. Bright-eyed Shelley brought in a fluttering lark which burst into the song of Chaucer's chanticleer. Henry Esmond gave his hand in a stately minuet to Diana of the Crossways. He evidently did not understand her nineteenth century wit; for he did not laugh. Perhaps he had lost his taste for clever women. Anon Dante and Swedenborg came together conversing earnestly about things remote and mystical. Swedenborg said it was very warm. Dante replied that it might rain in the night.

Suddenly there was a great clamour, and I found that "The Battle of the Books" had begun raging anew. Two figures entered in lively dispute. One was dressed in plain homespun and the other wore a scholar's gown over a suit of motley. I gathered from their conversation that they were Cotton Mather and William Shakspere. Mather insisted that the witches in "Macbeth" should be caught and hanged. Shakspere replied that the witches had already suffered enough at the hands of commentators. They were pushed aside by the twelve knights of the Round Table, who marched in bearing on a salver the goose that laid golden eggs. "The Pope's Mule" and "The Golden Bull" had a combat of history and fiction such as I had read of in books, but never before witnessed. These little animals were put to rout by a huge elephant which lumbered in with Rudyard Kipling riding high on its trunk. The elephant changed suddenly to "a rakish craft." (I do not know what a rakish craft is; but this was very rakish and very crafty.) It must have been abandoned long ago by wild pirates of the southern seas; for clinging to the rigging, and jovially cheering as the ship went down, I made out a man with blazing eyes, clad in a velveteen jacket. As the ship disappeared from sight, Falstaff rushed to the rescue of the lonely navigator—and stole his purse! But Miranda persuaded him to give it back. Stevenson said, "Who steals my purse steals trash." Falstaff laughed and called this a good joke, as good as any he had heard in his day.

This was the signal for a rushing swarm of quotations. They surged to and fro, an inchoate throng of half finished phrases, mutilated sentences, parodied sentiments, and brilliant metaphors. I could not distinguish any phrases or ideas of my own making. I saw a poor, ragged, shrunken sentence that might have been mine own catch the wings of a fair idea with the light of genius shining like a halo about its head.

Ever and anon the dancers changed partners without invitation or permission. Thoughts fell in love at sight, married in a measure, and joined hands without previous courtship. An incongruity is the wedding of two thoughts which have had no reasonable courtship, and marriages without wooing are apt to lead to domestic discord, even to the breaking up of an ancient, time-honoured family. Among the wedded couples were certain similes hitherto inviolable in their bachelorhood and spinsterhood, and held in great respect. Their extraordinary proceedings nearly broke up the dance. But the fatuity of their union was evident to them, and they parted. Other similes seemed to have the habit of living in discord. They had been many times married and divorced. They belonged to the notorious society of Mixed Metaphors.

A company of phantoms floated in and out wearing tantalizing garments of oblivion. They seemed about to dance, then vanished. They reappeared half a dozen times, but never unveiled their faces. The imp Curiosity pulled Memory by the sleeve and said, "Why do they run away? 'Tis strange knavery!" Out ran Memory to capture them. After a great deal of racing and puffing and collision it apprehended some of the fugitives and brought them in. But when it tore off their masks, lo! some were disappointingly commonplace, and others were gipsy quotations trying to conceal the punctuation marks that belonged to them. Memory was much chagrined to have had such a hard chase only to catch this sorry lot of graceless rogues.

Into the rabble strode four stately giants who called themselves History, Philosophy, Law, and Medicine. They seemed too solemn and imposing to join in a masque. But even as I gazed at these formidable guests, they all split into fragments which went whirling, dancing in divisions, subdivisions, re-subdivisions of scientific nonsense! History split into philology, ethnology, anthropology, and mythology, and these again split finer than the splitting of hairs. Each speciality hugged its bit of knowledge and waltzed it round and round. The rest of the company began to nod, and I felt drowsy myself. To put an end to the solemn gyrations, a troop of fairies mercifully waved poppies over us all, the masque faded, my head fell, and I started. Sleep had wakened me. At my elbow I found my old friend Bottom.

"Bottom," I said, "I have had a dream past the wit of man to say what dream it was. Methought I was—there is no man can tell what. The eye of man hath not heard, the ear of man hath not seen, his hand is not able to taste, his tongue to conceive, nor his heart to report what my dream was."

A Chant Of Darkness

"My wings are folded o'er mine ears,
My wings are crossèd o'er mine eyes,
Yet through their silver shade appears,
And through their lulling plumes arise,
A Shape, a throng of sounds."
Shelley's "Prometheus Unbound."

I DARE NOT ask why we are reft of light,
Banished to our solitary isles amid the unmeasured seas,
Or how our sight was nurtured to glorious vision,
To fade and vanish and leave us in the dark alone.
The secret of God is upon our tabernacle;
Into His mystery I dare not pry. Only this I know:
With Him is strength, with Him is wisdom,
And His wisdom hath set darkness in our paths.
Out of the uncharted, unthinkable dark we came,
And in a little time we shall return again
Into the vast, unanswering dark.

O Dark! thou awful, sweet, and holy Dark!
In thy solemn spaces, beyond the human eye,
God fashioned His universe; laid the foundations of the earth,
Laid the measure thereof, and stretched the line upon it;
Shut up the sea with doors, and made the glory
Of the clouds a covering for it;
Commanded His morning, and, behold! chaos fled
Before the uplifted face of the sun;
Divided a water-course for the overflowing of waters;
Sent rain upon the earth—
Upon the wilderness wherein there was no man,
Upon the desert where grew no tender herb,
And, lo! there was greenness upon the plains,
And the hills were clothed with beauty!
Out of the uncharted, unthinkable dark we came,
And in a little time we shall return again
Into the vast, unanswering dark.

O Dark! thou secret and inscrutable Dark!
In thy silent depths, the springs whereof man hath not
    fathomed,
God wrought the soul of man.
O Dark! compassionate, all-knowing Dark!
Tenderly, as shadows to the evening, comes thy message to
    man.
Softly thou layest thy hand on his tired eyelids,
And his soul, weary and homesick, returns
Unto thy soothing embrace.
Out of the uncharted, unthinkable dark we came,
And in a little time we shall return again
Into the vast, unanswering dark.

O Dark! wise, vital, thought-quickening Dark!
In thy mystery thou hidest the light
That is the soul's life.
Upon thy solitary shores I walk unafraid;
I dread no evil; though I walk in the valley of the shadow,
I shall not know the ecstasy of fear
When gentle Death leads me through life's open door,
When the bands of night are sundered,
And the day outpours its light.
Out of the uncharted, unthinkable dark we came,
And in a little time we shall return again
Into the vast, unanswering dark.

The timid soul, fear-driven, shuns the dark;
But upon the cheeks of him who must abide in shadow
Breathes the wind of rushing angel-wings,
And round him falls a light from unseen fires.
Magical beams glow athwart the darkness;
Paths of beauty wind through his black world
To another world of light,
Where no veil of sense shuts him out from Paradise.
Out of the uncharted, unthinkable dark we came,
And in a little time we shall return again
Into the vast, unanswering dark.

O Dark! thou blessèd, quiet Dark!
To the lone exile who must dwell with thee
Thou art benign and friendly;

From the harsh world thou dost shut him in;
To him thou whisperest the secrets of the wondrous night;
Upon him thou bestowest regions wide and boundless as his spirit;
Thou givest a glory to all humble things;
With thy hovering pinions thou coverest all unlovely objects;
Under thy brooding wings there is peace.
Out of the uncharted, unthinkable dark we came,
And in a little time we shall return again
Into the vast, unanswering dark.

II
Once in regions void of light I wandered;
In blank darkness I stumbled,
And fear led me by the hand;
My feet pressed earthward,
Afraid of pitfalls.
By many shapeless terrors of the night affrighted,
To the wakeful day
I held out beseeching arms.

Then came Love, bearing in her hand
The torch that is the light unto my feet,
And softly spoke Love: "Hast thou
Entered into the treasures of darkness?
[Hast thou entered into the treasures of the night?
Search out thy blindness. It holdeth
Riches past computing."

The words of Love set my spirit aflame.
My eager fingers searched out the mysteries,
The splendours, the inmost sacredness, of things,
And in the vacancies discerned
With spiritual sense the fullness of life;
And the gates of Day stood wide.

I am shaken with gladness;
My limbs tremble with joy;
My heart and the earth
Tremble with happiness;
The ecstasy of life

Is abroad in the world.
Knowledge hath uncurtained heaven;
On the uttermost shores of darkness there is light;
Midnight hath sent forth a beam!
The blind that stumbled in darkness without light
Behold a new day!
In the obscurity gleams the star of Thought;
Imagination hath a luminous eye,
And the mind hath a glorious vision.

III
"The man is blind. What is life to him?
A closed book held up against a sightless face.
Would that he could see
Yon beauteous star, and know
For one transcendent moment
The palpitating joy of sight!"

All sight is of the soul.
Behold it in the upward flight
Of the unfettered spirit! Hast thou seen
Thought bloom in the blind child's face?
Hast thou seen his mind grow,
Like the running dawn, to grasp
The vision of the Master?
It was the miracle of inward sight.

In the realms of wonderment where I dwell
I explore life with my hands;
I recognize, and am happy;
My fingers are ever athirst for the earth,
And drink up its wonders with delight,
Draw out earth's dear delights;
My feet are charged with the murmur,
The throb, of all things that grow.

This is touch, this quivering,
This flame, this ether,
This glad rush of blood,
This daylight in my heart,
This glow of sympathy in my palms!
Thou blind, loving, all-prying touch,

Thou openest the book of life to me.
The noiseless little noises of the earth
Come with softest rustle;
The shy, sweet feet of life;
The silky mutter of moth-wings
Against my restraining palm;
The strident beat of insect-wings,
The silvery trickle of water;
Little breezes busy in the summer grass;
The music of crisp, whisking, scurrying leaves,
The swirling, wind-swept, frost-tinted leaves;
The crystal splash of summer rain,
Saturate with the odours of the sod.

With alert fingers I listen
To the showers of sound
That the wind shakes from the forest.
I bathe in the liquid shade
Under the pines, where the air hangs cool

After the shower is done.
My saucy little friend the squirrel
Flips my shoulder with his tail,
Leaps from leafy billow to leafy billow,
Returns to eat his breakfast from my hand.
Between us there is glad sympathy;
He gambols; my pulses dance;
I am exultingly full of the joy of life!

Have not my fingers split the sand
On the sun-flooded beach?
Hath not my naked body felt the water sing
When the sea hath enveloped it
With rippling music?
Have I not felt
The lilt of waves beneath my boat,
The flap of sail,
The strain of mast,
The wild rush
Of the lightning-charged winds?
Have I not smelt the swift, keen flight
Of winged odours before the tempest?
Here is joy awake, aglow;

A CHANT OF DARKNESS

Here is the tumult of the heart.
My hands evoke sight and sound out of feeling,
Intershifting the senses endlessly;
Linking motion with sight, odour with sound
They give colour to the honeyed breeze,
The measure and passion of a symphony
To the beat and quiver of unseen wings.
In the secrets of earth and sun and air
My fingers are wise;
They snatch light out of darkness,
They thrill to harmonies breathed in silence.

I walked in the stillness of the night,
And my soul uttered her gladness.
O Night, still, odorous Night, I love thee!
O wide, spacious Night, I love thee!
O steadfast, glorious Night!
I touch thee with my hands;
I lean against thy strength;
I am comforted.

O fathomless, soothing Night!
Thou art a balm to my restless spirit,
I nestle gratefully in thy bosom,
Dark, gracious mother!
Like a dove, I rest in thy bosom.
Out of the uncharted, unthinkable dark we came,
And in a little time we shall return again
Into the vast, unanswering dark.

Made in the USA
Monee, IL
09 December 2020